SHELLEY'S *FRANKENSTEIN*

CONTINUUM READER'S GUIDES

Achebe's Things Fall Apart – Ode Ogede

Austen's Emma – Gregg A. Hecimovich

Chaucer's The Canterbury Tales – Gail Ashton

Conrad's Heart of Darkness – Allan Simmons

Dickens's Great Expectations – Ian Brinton

Eliot's Middlemarch – Josie Billington

Fitzgerald's The Great Gatsby – Nicolas Tredell

Fowles's The French Lieutenant's Woman – William Stephenson

Salinger's The Catcher in the Rye – Sarah Graham

William Blake's Poetry – Jonathan Roberts

SHELLEY'S
FRANKENSTEIN

GRAHAM ALLEN

continuum

Continuum International Publishing Group
The Tower Building
11 York Road
London
SE1 7NX

80 Maiden Lane
Suite 704
New York
NY 10038

British Library Cataloging-in-Publication Data
A catalogue record for this book is available from the British Library.

ISBN: 978-0-8264-9524-2 (Hardback)
978-0-8264-9525-9 (Paperback)

Library of Congress Cataloging-in-Publication Data
A catalog record for this book is available from the Library of Congress.

Typeset by Servis Filmsetting Ltd, Stockport, Cheshire
Printed and bound in Great Britain by
MPG Books Ltd, Bodmin, Cornwall

For Gary Baker, my 'brother' and most enduring friend.

CONTENTS

NOTES ON SOURCES

Full publication details for all works cited can be found in the final chapter, 'Further Reading'. After an initial list of editions of *Frankenstein*, other works by Mary Shelley, and a selected list of works on Mary Shelley, this chapter is arranged thematically in line with Chapters 1 to 5. Unless otherwise specified references are to the first edition of the novel (1818), cross-referenced for the convenience of readers with the Broadview Press 1818 text, 2nd ed., edited by D. L. Macdonald and Kathleen Scherf (1999) (hereafter cited as B). References to the Thomas, 1823 and 1831 versions are taken from B. or from *Frankenstein*, ed. Nora Crook. vol. 1, *The Novels and Selected Works of Mary Shelley*, gen. eds. Nora Crook with Pamela Clemit, consulting ed. Betty T. Bennett, 8 vols, London: Pickering and Chatto, 1996.

CHAPTER 1

CONTEXTS

Frankenstein; Or The Modern Prometheus, first published in 1818, is one of the most influential literary texts to have been written in English. It is a novel which is deeply embedded in that cultural and political period we call Romantic, and has been described by William St Clair as Romanticism's most persistently influential literary work (St Clair, *The Reading Nation*, p. 357). From its first publication, however, *Frankenstein* was more than just another novel, and Chris Baldick has rightly called it 'a modern myth' (Baldick, p. 1). There appears to be something about *Frankenstein* which encourages every generation to read it in terms of their historically specific anxieties and obsessions. The mythic element of *Frankenstein*, as Baldick explains, resides in this incitement to re-reading and revision, and in what it produces: 'That series of adaptations, allusions, accretions, analogues, parodies, and plain misreadings which follows upon Mary Shelley's novel is not just a supplementary component of the myth; it *is* the myth' (Baldick, p. 4). From the earliest moralizing reviews and theatrical adaptations, through a century of allusions and retellings into the filmic and televisual obsession with the text in the twentieth and twenty-first centuries, it would appear that *Frankenstein* has been a text (a story, an idea, a series of images and narrative set pieces) which has provided British, European and, increasingly, global cultures with ways of examining and explaining themselves. The distance between such re-readings and the original text (or texts) of the novel can become strikingly large, so that many readers (saturated with cultural references to Shelley's most famous work) can find the novel itself, when they finally read it, rather surprising and unexpectedly detached from its numerous cultural versions.

When students are confronted with *Frankenstein*, they are immediately faced with questions that go to the very heart of literary and cultural studies. The most pressing questions concern whether or not readers should attempt to return to the original text and its immediate historical contexts, or whether they should address the many meanings the novel has provoked throughout what is now almost two centuries of reception. *Frankenstein*, as we will see, was published in various editions. Mary Shelley altered a significant portion of the novel for the 1831 Standard Novels edition. *Frankenstein*, then, is not a singular entity. There is no single, stable text to which we can return. Even if we decide, as readers, that we wish to return to the 'true' (original, authentic, authorially intended) *Frankenstein*, we discover we have to negotiate between texts and, as Chapter 4 will also explain, even between authors. As Fred Botting has suggested, there is something about *Frankenstein* that radically foregrounds the often hidden but still active desire for mastery in traditional forms of literary criticism. The story's focus on how the desire for mastery leads to the production of, and conflict with, monstrous doubles is played out again, Botting suggests, in every attempt to master the meaning of Shelley's text critically (Botting, *Making Monstrous*, p. 5).

Reading *Frankenstein* involves us in an education about monsters. We may begin by imagining monsters on a purely Gothic level (huge lumbering figures of the Boris Karloff type); the novel, however, very quickly teaches us that monsters also exist on the psychological, the ethical and the politico-social level. Many of *Frankenstein*'s modern readers have explored the relationship the novel draws between monsters and the social process of *othering*. This process of *othering*, of making monstrous (to use Botting's phrase), can involve aspects of life and the world which are psychical, social, sexual, ethnic, class-based. Those in positions of power (masters), so such readings contend, inevitably attempt to *other* (turn into images of the non-human, or the inauthentic or illegitimate) those aspects of society and human life which

2

threaten the dominant social order. At the very centre of the text, of course, the creature himself goes through this education about monsters, not only learning of how his own creator had *othered* him, but even more tragically how such processes of repression and distortion seem inescapable within human history and human social systems. Having listened to Felix read Volney's *Ruins of Empire* (1791) to Safie, the Christian-Arab girl who seeks protection in the De Lacey home, the creature reflects on the ambivalent nature of humanity, and on how what is great and glorious in the human sphere always appears to be achieved at the cost of a monstrous *othering* of those outside of the realms of power and influence:

> These wonderful narrations inspired me with strange feelings. Was man, indeed, at once so powerful, so virtuous, and magnificent, yet so vicious and base? He appeared at one time a mere scion of the evil principle, and at another as all that can be conceived of noble and godlike. To be a great and virtuous man appeared the highest honour that can befall a sensitive being; to be base and vicious, as many on record have been, appeared the lowest degradation, a condition more abject than that of the blind mole or harmless worm. For a long time I could not conceive how one man could go forth to murder his fellow, or even why there were laws and governments; but when I heard details of vice and bloodshed, my wonder ceased, and I turned away with disgust and loathing. (*1818*, vol. 2, pp. 77–9; see B, pp. 144–5)

Frankenstein is a novel which explores the manner in which human beings create monsters and become monsters: it is also a novel which has become a myth-making monster which still, to this day, threatens to *other* its own creator, Mary Shelley. In her 1831 Introduction, Shelley playfully acknowledges the monstrous independence her novel appears to have gained in the world, but she also implicitly regrets the manner in which her textual creature has propelled a misreading of her own life and private emotions into the public arena. The myths produced by her most famous novel had, by the 1830s, also begun to contribute to a myth of Mary Shelley herself. In her Introduction, therefore, she once again attempts to separate the public life of her novel from her private life as the widow of the poet, P. B. Shelley:

> And now, once again, I bid my hideous progeny go forth and prosper. I have an affection for it, for it was the offspring of happy days, when death and grief were but words, which found no true echo in my heart. Its several pages speak of many a walk, many a drive, and many a conversation, when I was not alone; and my companion was one who, in this world, I shall never see more. But this is for myself; my readers have nothing to do with these associations. (B, p. 358)

The move Shelley is attempting here is rather complex and even contradictory. Attempting to separate her novel from her personal life and private grief, she reminds us of the relations that have been drawn between her novel and her private life before stating that there is no real relation. Her modern readers are confronted with the same contradictory procedure: in order to move beyond the biographical 'myth of Mary Shelley' (which has frequently distorted any adequate reception of *Frankenstein* and her many other literary and non-literary works) we have to remind ourselves of some of the details of her biography. As various readers have recognized, biographical readings of Shelley's works are extremely problematic (they tend to reinforce the 'myth' we are referring to here), and yet they are also, in many ways, unavoidable (see Allen, 'Beyond Biographism', and Gillingham; see also Sunstein, pp. 401–3).

BIOGRAPHICAL BACKGROUND

Mary Shelley was the daughter of two of the most significant radical writers and thinkers of the earlier decades of the Romantic period, a period dominated by political, social and artistic reactions to the American and then the French Revolutions. The 1790s, in which Shelley was born (30 August 1797, to be precise), have been labelled by Marilyn Butler as the revolutionary decade, a decade in British cultural and intellectual life dominated by what she also calls 'the revolution controversy'. Shelley's father, William Godwin, was a proponent of social reform based on a philosophical and political account of reason, most thoroughly extrapolated in the various editions of his *Enquiry Concerning Political Justice and its Influence on Morals and Happiness* (1793, 1796, 1798). Mary Wollstonecraft, who died days after giving birth to her daughter Mary, was the author of various reformist texts, including her proto-feminist work of educational and social theory, *A Vindication of the Rights of Woman* (1792). Mary met her future husband, the already notorious aristocratic poet, P. B. Shelley, because he was paying a disciple's visit to the great Godwin, widower of the equally admired Wollstonecraft. In dedicatory verses to Mary at the beginning of his *Laon and Cythna* (1817), P. B. Shelley calls Mary 'Child of love and light', before going on to define her beauty (both intellectual and physical) in terms of her relations to her parents. It seems to have been Mary's fate always to have been judged in terms of her relations to others:

They say that thou wert lovely from thy birth,
Of glorious parents, thou aspiring Child.
I wonder not – for One then left this earth
Whose life was like tae setting planet mild,
Which clothed thee in the radiance undefiled
Of its departing glory; still her fame
Shines on thee, through the tempests dark and wild
Which shake these latter days; and thou canst claim
The shelter, from thy Sire, of an immortal name.
(P. B. Shelley, *Poems*, vol. 2, p. 56)

The 'immortal name' P. B. Shelley is referring to in the last line is that of Mary's father, Godwin. One can read these lines as implying a subtle, Oedipal reversal of power, however, with P. B. Shelley's 'immortal name' replacing that of Godwin, the protection now being 'from thy Sire'. Given the life they led after eloping in 1814 (accompanied by her stepsister, Claire Clairmont), one cannot but wonder whether the name of Shelley ever provided Mary with anything we might describe as a 'shelter'? P. B. Shelley was, when he ran off to the continent with Mary and Claire, still a married man. The elopement was to have huge consequences for those immediately involved and for many others. Mary's half-sister, Fanny Imlay, committed suicide in October 1816, two months later the poet's first wife, Harriet Westbrook, also took her life; a Chancery Court decision of 1817 denied P. B. Shelley the right to bring up his children (Ianthe and Charles) from his first marriage. The Shelleys were themselves to lose three children, the first after only a few weeks in 1815, Clara and William in Italy between 1818 and 1819. By the time P. B. Shelley drowned in 1822, Mary Shelley seemed to some of her circle to have lost her youth and her belief in the political and philosophical ideals of her parents and her husband.

Mary Shelley's reputation as an author has, until very recently, been dictated by two facts: she was the 'Author of *Frankenstein*' and 'The Wife of P. B. Shelley'. The latter meant that from 1822, if not before, Mary Shelley became part of the attempt to turn the life and work of P. B. Shelley into a modern myth. Writers such as Leigh Hunt, Edward Trelawny, Thomas Medwin and Thomas Jefferson Hogg, started a process which transformed P. B. Shelley into an 'ineffectual angel', too pure and too good for the corrupt world in which he had so briefly lived. Leigh Hunt, in his *Autobiography*, wrote: 'He was like a spirit that had darted out of its orb, and found itself in another world. I used to tell him that he had come from the planet Mercury' (Hunt, p. 331). Mary Shelley, the rightful executor and editor of her husband's literary legacy, was often viewed as an obstacle in the way of the construction of the Shelley myth. As a consequence, many of P. B. Shelley's biographers and literary supporters found it convenient to write off his wife as an unworthy, essentially conventional woman, who, after the poet died, lapsed into modes of conservatism which were essentially a betrayal of the poet's ideals. Trelawny, self-appointed biographer of the Byron–Shelley circle, is perhaps the most conspicuous peddler of such an account of Mary Shelley, and throughout his many versions of the life and death of P. B. Shelley he paints an ever bleaker version of her lack of intellectual and emotional sympathy. In an appendix added to his *Records of Shelley, Byron, and the Author* in 1878, Trelawny states that she 'had little or no sympathy with any of her husband's theories; she could not but admire the great capacity and learning of her husband, but she had no faith in his views, and she grieved that he was so stubborn and inflexible' (Trelawny, *Records*, p. 300). At the beginning of this appended character sketch, Trelawny articulates the twin poles of the Mary Shelley myth in so concise and authoritative a way that it can read (and indeed did read to many) like fact: 'Her capacity can be judged by the novels she wrote after Shelley's death, more than ordinarily commonplace and conventional. Whilst overshadowed by Shelley's greatness her faculties expanded; but when she had lost him they shrank into their natural littleness' (Trelawny, *Records*, p. 299). This from a man who had allowed Mary Shelley to see his fictional biography, *Adventures of a Younger Son* (1831), through the press and who was close enough to her in the early 1830s for marriage to be broached, even if it was not clear by whom (see Seymour, p. 419). In Trelawny's account we have that image of Mary Shelley as a young woman, so inspired by her association with P. B. Shelley that she was able to write the unquestionably profound and dynamic novel *Frankenstein*, and as an older woman, mourning the loss of her genius husband, turning out substandard novels, as conventional and trivial as herself. In this mythical reading of Mary Shelley's life and work, *Frankenstein* becomes the product not of its author's own literary skill, but rather of a kind of psychical and creative osmosis, or temporary vitalization. Mary Shelley wrote above herself when she wrote *Frankenstein*, so the myth goes, because in that period of her life she stood close to male, literary genius. We can find this myth of the temporarily inspired wife still active throughout the critical reception of *Frankenstein* and Shelley's other work, as here in Richard Church's 1928 account:

> She continued to devote herself to her son, and to her literary work. Very little of the latter has survived the criticisms of Time, for the reason that it was all no more than variations on a single spiritual theme. *Frankenstein*, inspired by her contact with Shelley and Byron during the memorable holiday on the

lake of Geneva, is the only book which has won a permanent place in English fiction. (Church, p. 90)

Remembering the 1831 Introduction, we have to recognize that even Shelley herself was capable of contributing to this myth of temporary inspiration when she attributes the origin of her story to listening to Byron and P. B. Shelley discuss scientific matters. She begins an important paragraph on contemporary scientific debates: 'Many and long were the conversations between Lord Byron and Shelley, to which I was a devout but nearly silent listener' (B, p. 356). By the time Shelley wrote her Introduction, however, she had returned from Italy to England a widow, financially dependent on her less than sympathetic father-in-law, Sir Timothy Shelley. The poet's father was appalled by his son's public notoriety; P. B. Shelley had been expelled from Oxford University for writing a tract entitled *The Necessity of Atheism*, and had been, throughout his writing life, the target of the conservative press and literary reviewers. Sir Timothy Shelley, who had initially demanded that Mary hand over to him her one remaining son, Percy Florence, doled out limited funds to his daughter-in-law (for the upbringing of his grandson) on the strict understanding that she forego her plans to publish her husband's work and write his biography. The world within which Mary Shelley lived and wrote, after 1823 when she returned to England, was a constrained and somewhat prohibitive one. Surrounded by people who believed they knew her lost husband as well as she (and were often willing to assert such ideas publicly), her hands tied by the resentful and tenacious Sir Timothy (he did not die until 1844), and, as Betty T. Bennett has noted, domesticated by the reviewers who could not understand that a woman writer could produce anything more than 'romance' novels, the remarkable truth about Mary Shelley's life is that she managed to write so much and to remain so consistent in her own unique version of reformist politics. In the past three decades, because of the work of scholars such as Bennett, Pamela Clemit, Nora Crook and Charles E. Robinson, readers have begun to be able to step outside of the myth of Mary Shelley, and understand the manner in which *Frankenstein* is not a one-off, an aberration and literary cul-de-sac, but rather the opening text in the literary career of one of the most intellectually and artistically gifted writers of the first four decades of the nineteenth century.

RE-EVALUATING MARY SHELLEY

Shelley wrote a huge amount of fictional and non-fictional work between 1818 and the beginning of the 1840s, much of which has only been available to readers outside of major libraries in the past few decades (for brief but very useful accounts of the recent re-evaluation of Shelley's work see Crook, 'Introduction', and Clemit in O'Neill). Shelley's six other major fictional works are at once impressively diverse and yet consistent in their development of themes already vitally present within *Frankenstein*. They also demonstrate narrative and literary techniques which recur so frequently that they can be said to form part of her authorial signature or voice. Whether presenting historical fictions like *Valperga* (1823) or *Perkin Warbeck* (1830), or more contemporaneous studies of familial and social relations like *Mathilda* (composed 1819–20), *Lodore* (1835) and *Falkner* (1837), Shelley's major fictional works all display a narrative complexity and an intertextual density which have, until recently, remained unobserved by most of her readers, antagonistic and sympathetic alike. These works, along with her letters, journals, travel writing, short stories and a significant amount of historical and biographical writing, also display a consistent commitment to the reformist ideals Shelley shared with her parents and her husband. To share key principles, hopes and aspirations need not, however, imply complete agreement. Shelley's reformist politics were, throughout her life, of a 'realist' tendency. Shelley was not a 'realist' in terms of novelistic form, nor perhaps in the stricter senses of that word in the discipline of philosophy; the word does adequately mark, however, her inability to believe that the negative sides of life could be eradicated by the exercise of reason. This is a crucial point and one which, if we understand it and observe its force in her entire literary oeuvre, tells us fundamental things about her first, most famous novel.

In her editorial comments, which she presented in her 1839 edition of P. B. Shelley's *Poetical Works*, Mary Shelley frequently distanced herself from the more 'idealist' views of her husband. The following passage from her 'Note on *Prometheus Unbound*' is an example:

> The prominent feature of Shelley's theory of the destiny of the human species was, that evil is not inherent in the system of the creation, but an accident that might be expelled. This also forms a portion of Christianity; God made earth and man perfect, till he, by his fall,
>
> 'Brought death into the world and all our woe.'
>
> Shelley believed that mankind had only to will that there should be no evil, and there would be none. It is not my part in these notes to notice the arguments that have been urged against this opinion, but to mention the fact that he entertained it, and was indeed attached to it with fervent enthusiasm. (Mary Shelley, *Novels*, vol. 2, p. 277)

It is unnecessary for Mary Shelley to state that she does not share her husband's beautiful 'enthusiasm'; the fact that she does not rings out loud and clear. This is not, however, confirmation of a lapse into conventionality and political conservatism in her later work. Mary Shelley had never believed in the doctrine that 'mankind had only to will that there should be no evil, and there would be none'. Throughout her writing she displays a caution when confronted with arguments which assert that human beings have a potentially complete control over themselves and the world in which they live.

Godwin's fundamental belief in the power of reason often led him in his writings to assert something close to this limitless control (at least *in potentia*), and it is precisely his notion of Necessity that the young disciple, P. B. Shelley, was to take up in poems such as *Queen Mab* (1813). Godwin's account of Necessity is a complex one and can be found in *Political Justice* and elsewhere (see Philp, pp. 89–96). Essentially the doctrine asserts that the human ethical realm functions in the same way (according to the same laws of cause and effect) as does the natural world. We understand nature through the law of Necessity (through our understanding of cause and effect), and, so says Godwin, if we only learn to exercise our rational faculties we can come to have the same understanding of the realm of ethical and social events. Godwin's most famous and controversial example of his doctrine of Necessity comes in the beginning of the second book of *Political Justice*, when he argues that if the palace of the great French political philosopher Fénelon were in flames, and one could save only one person, it would be rational to save Fénelon rather than his chambermaid, even if the chambermaid were 'my wife, my mother or my benefactor' (Godwin, *Political*, vol. 3, p. 50; for the second edition version of this section of *Political Justice*, see B, pp. 252–4). The point Godwin is trying to make is a quasi-utilitarian one, in which whenever we are confronted with an ethical choice, reason always allows us to make an informed estimate of what will bring the greater good to the greatest amount of people. Fénelon will bring greater good to the world than the chambermaid if he is saved, thus a person's actions in such a situation can be established on the principle of Necessity, or a kind of causal logic of moral action.

One can see Mary Shelley's critique of such notions throughout her writings. In *Mathilda*, a text in which a guilty father commits suicide and a daughter finally expires after having found no way out of her all-embracing melancholia, Shelley writes of '[t]he chain of necessity ever bringing misery' and 'the malignant fate that presides over' the world (Mary Shelley, *Novels*, vol. 2, p. 49). In her next major novel, *Valperga*, Shelley contrasts a female character, Euthanasia, who embodies the Enlightenment ideals of education and reason, with a male character, the historical Castruccio Castracani, who increasingly comes to embody that malignant version of Necessity figured in the above passage from *Mathilda*. Euthanasia may linger in the reader's mind, as a beautiful exemplum of the best qualities of the human mind, but it is Castruccio who defeats all who oppose him, before he too, at the very end, dies with no meaningful legacy to bequeath. In her third novel, *The Last Man* (1826), Shelley takes her negative, counter-version of Necessity to an extreme, and presents the story of how a pandemic wipes the human race from the earth. These texts can appear excessively negative, and there is no wonder that even some of Shelley's most sophisticated readers have come to the conclusion that her works express a consistently anti-Enlightenment, anti-reformist agenda (see, for example, Jane Blumberg). The fact of the matter is that Mary Shelley shared a belief in the reformist politics of her circle, as is demonstrated by her letters, her journals, and her fictional and non-fictional work. From the very beginning, however, Shelley's life had been such that she could not share in the idea of a law of Necessity which, if only human beings exercised their reason, could eradicate tragedy from the social world and establish humanity on a road towards what Godwin called perfectibility. Mary Shelley's fictional and non-fictional work is 'realist'; it balances the greatest qualities of human beings against the ineradicable presence of tragedy within human life. Her work is, in this respect, deeply complex, requiring serious and sustained interpretation. Often, as in *The Last Man*, but also later novels like *Lodore* and *Falkner*, Shelley presents novels which seem to move in two opposing directions, offering a bleak literal scenario subtly undercut by a reaffirmation of Enlightenment principles of reason, education, equality and sincerity between social classes and between the sexes. In these later novels, despite having a greater surface veneer of conventionality, we find texts which are thoroughly imbued with a recognition of the ambivalence of human life and human aspirations. It is this recognition of ambivalence in human life, along with Shelley's commitment to and yet realistic assessment of the Enlightenment reformism of her circle, that, once understood, can lead us back to a more informed and balanced reading of *Frankenstein*.

FRANKENSTEIN AND THE AGE OF REVOLUTION

Frankenstein, as many recent critics have demonstrated, presents a radical re-imagining of major symbols and figures inherited from the revolutionary debates of the 1790s and early 1800s. This language is full of monsters, masters and slaves, Promethean rebels and tyrannical, or at least unsympathetic, creator gods. Chris Baldick's discussion of the manner in which the novel stages the language of 'the revolution controversy' is still the most compelling. Moving through the use of such language in the anti-revolution work of Edmund Burke, along with its presence in more radical writers like Godwin, Wollstonecraft and Tom Paine, Baldick attempts to sum up the manner in which *Frankenstein* appears to support both the conservative, Burkean and the more reformist uses of these established figures:

> Telling the story of a monster out of the control of its philosophical creator, *Frankenstein* reanimates recognizably the terms of the debate over the French Revolution. As Lee Sterrenburg has argued, the monster is derived from the lurid imagery of Burke's counter-revolutionary polemics, but manages at the same time to voice the opposing views of Mary Wollstonecraft and others, indicating the prevailing system from the standpoint of the oppressed and outcast. The mythically productive equivocation of *Frankenstein* appears to emerge ultimately from this double – indeed contradictory – derivation from contending political positions. (Baldick, p. 54)

If *Frankenstein* is a response to 'the revolution controversy', then, critics such as Baldick have asked, does it take a conservative or radical line? If readers focus on the narrative of the creature, they might answer that it takes a distinctly radical line, exploring the manner in which an understandable desire for revenge and retribution is generated within the minds of society's 'monsters'. If they focus on Victor as a figure of the Enlightenment (the age of Reason) which produced the ideas behind the French Revolution, they may well end up, as Sterrenberg and many other readers have, taking the opposite view. Recent interest in the origins of the secret society of the Illuminati at the University of Ingolstadt (the university Victor attends), and the history of its creation of the 'monster' of the French Revolution in the Abbé Barruel's *Mémoires pour server à l'histoire du Jacobinisme* (1797), has led a series of critics to ponder whether *Frankenstein* adopts Barruel's conservative critique of revolution or whether it secretly attempts to reverse it. The Shelleys read Barruel's book in 1814 (Mary Shelley,

Journals, pp. 18–19). Discussions of this interesting influence (Paulson, Ketterer, Clemit *Godwinian Novel*, Sterrenburg, Scott, Dart) merely deepens the impression that on a political level *Frankenstein* can be interpreted in opposing, even contradictory directions.

Baldick's view is that the novel equivocates, that it does not come down on either of the opposing sides of the debate. In that political equivocation Baldick finds the primary source of the powerful and enduring myth that *Frankenstein* has created. Put simply, Baldick's reading explains how *Frankenstein* generated an enduring socio-cultural myth by allowing readers to use it for competing ideological purposes. In 1824, only a year after Mary Shelley had returned to England and attended a performance of Richard Brinsley Peake's adaptation of her novel (see Chapter 5), the British Foreign Secretary, George Canning, showed that Shelley's novel could be interpreted on conservative grounds by using *Frankenstein* to argue against the freeing of West Indian slaves (see Morton, p. 30 and Baldick, p. 60). We should remember, however, that radical Romantic writers, such as Blake and P. B. Shelley, had conflated Milton's Satan in *Paradise Lost* with the classical figure of Prometheus in order to explore the psychology and morality of the oppressed and enslaved classes and to thereby assert the need for forms of social revolution and reform. When the creature himself reads Milton's epic, his responses appear to contribute to that radical mode of Romantic Prometheanism: 'Many times I considered Satan as the fitter emblem of my condition; for often, like him, when I viewed the bliss of my protectors, the bitter gall of envy rose within me' (*1818*, vol. 2, p. 105; see B, p. 154). From this perspective, *Frankenstein* reads like another reformist call for greater social inclusion, another contribution to 'Promethean Romanticism'.

Baldick's reading, seminal as it is, seems to leave us with a Shelley who did not so much contribute to the political and social debates which raged around her as somewhat passively negotiate their influence. It gives us Mary Shelley the equivocator, Mary Shelley the influenced rather than the influencer. Such readings, against their intentions, perpetuate in subtle ways the myth of Mary Shelley as an author by default, an author who produced one stunning text because of her proximity to male agents, male thinkers and artists. The truth of the matter may be that we are only now beginning to understand that Shelley had her own quite distinctive contribution to make to the reformist politics and literature she inherited and so decisively affected. That contribution comes in her 'realist' assessment of the reformist politics of the circle she was born into, lived within and ultimately outlived. The next step in understanding this contribution is to remember the particularities of the novel form Shelley inherited from her father and mother.

STUDY QUESTIONS

1. In the 1831 Introduction to *Frankenstein*, Mary Shelley appears to be attempting to contain and even tame the relationship that had been established between her private life and her most famous novel. Can you find other examples in her Introduction which demonstrate Shelley's anxiety over the presentation of the biography of her own life and those of her circle.

2. In this opening chapter I have made a case for Mary Shelley's 'realist' attitude towards the Enlightenment, perfectibilist ideas she inherited from her father and her husband. Can you find instances in the novel which appear to confirm Shelley's belief that human reason cannot simply eradicate tragedy from the world?

CHAPTER 2

LANGUAGE, FORM AND STYLE

In this chapter we will be concentrating on the generic form of *Frankenstein*, its relation to the novel tradition associated with Mary Shelley's parents, William Godwin and Mary Wollstonecraft. In Chapter 3 we will employ the contexts discussed here in analysing other aspects of form and style, including *Frankenstein*'s frame narrative and use of multiple narrators, along with the complex network of imagery the novel presents to its readers. We should begin, however, by highlighting some general features of its language, form and style.

When modern readers not familiar with the Romantic novel come to read *Frankenstein* they are frequently surprised by the rather elaborate, 'literary' and historically dated nature of its language. *Frankenstein* has created such an enduring and omnipresent myth that readers can be surprised by the antiquated manner in which many of its characters speak and write. When narrating his and Clerval's route through Britain, in Volume 3, Chapter Two, Victor writes the following:

> I visited Edinburgh with languid eyes and mind; and yet that city might have interested the most unfortunate being. Clerval did not like it so well as Oxford; for the antiquity of the latter city was more pleasing to him. But the beauty and regularity of the new town of Edinburgh, its romantic castle, and its environs, the most delightful in the world, Arthur's Seat, St. Bernard's Well, and the Pentland Hills, compensated him for the change, and filled him with cheerfulness and

admiration. But I was impatient to arrive at the termination of my journey. (*1818*, vol. 3, pp. 32–3; B, p. 187).

The passage is not the most conspicuous example of the kind of language I have just been referring to; in fact, it presents us with Victor Frankenstein in his most factual and circumstantial mode of writing. Modern readers, however, will inevitably find the manner in which he uses words such as 'termination', 'languid', 'compensated' and 'environs' indicators of an historically specific idiom of English. Anne Mellor has argued that P. B. Shelley's involvement in the drafting and copying of the text of *Frankenstein* introduced into it a intensified level of literary 'formality'. She writes: 'Percy is clearly responsible for much of the most inflated rhetoric in the text' (Mellor, *Mary Shelley*, p. 61). In other parts of her study, however, Mellor argues that P. B. Shelley's revisions to the 1818 *Frankenstein* clearly improved the text. P. B. Shelley's involvement in the composition of *Frankenstein* is a complex matter; we will discuss it in Chapter 4. What is important here is that the novel is an example of the historically specific phenomenon of Romantic fiction. Aspects of the language presented in *Frankenstein* have, of course, become antiquated. We need also to remember, however, that in its multiple forms the Romantic novel did not always or even normally seek to generate the kind of linguistic 'naturalism' or 'realism' readers have become so familiar with since the rise of the classic Victorian novels of Charles Dickens or George Eliot. In this chapter we will see how Mary Shelley's use of intensified, at times hyperbolic, language relates her novel not only to the tradition of Gothic fiction, but also to her parents' psychological and political deployment of the language of Gothic novels.

If the language, style and tone of *Frankenstein* can seem somewhat antiquated for modern readers, the novel's heterogeneous mix of kinds of languages (what are often called social and cultural discourses) can make it seem a very modern, even postmodern text. It is a common observation that in postmodern art (since the 1960s) the once carefully guarded boundaries between popular and 'high' culture are rejected in favour of an eclectic style in which popular forms such as detective fiction are placed

17

side-by-side with echoes and allusions to classical literature and other indicators of 'high' culture. The novels of Umberto Eco are frequently cited examples of this point. *Frankenstein*, if we look at it from this perspective, can appear a very modern text. It mixes popular forms, such as the Gothic novel, with a series of 'high' cultural references to classical authors, for example Dante, Milton, Shakespeare and Plutarch. The creature's absorption of such classical texts, concealed in the 'hovel' by the impoverished De Lacey cottage, is an unforgettable emblem of this aspect of the novel. *Frankenstein* also weaves together a host of apparently exclusive, even antagonistic discourses: the modern scientific discourse of chemistry is blended, in Frankenstein's narrative, with the antique and mythic discourse of alchemy; scientific and religious discourses blend and clash in Victor Frankenstein's account of his life and work. When readers begin to look for the presence of such juxtaposed or antithetical discourses within *Frankenstein*, they discover that the novel is replete with examples, including, perhaps most importantly, discourses associated with the domestic and those associated with the political and public spheres. A merging – or at least a complex staging of the juxtaposition – between culturally feminine and masculine discourses appears to structure *Frankenstein* as a novel: feminine discourses concerned with family, love, the need for empathy and sympathy, are positioned beside discourses which emphasize a masculine quest for scientific and public renown, along with a need to sacrifice self and others for such quests. Characters also appear to transgress gender-specific discursive boundaries: Walton employs a form of communication (letter-writing) which, in the period, was frequently if not exclusively associated with feminine culture. It is Elizabeth, not Victor, who, during the trial of Justine Moritz, delivers a public ('masculine') defence of her 'cousin'.

The language, style and form of *Frankenstein* can appear outdated or extremely modern, even postmodern, depending upon the perspective we bring to it. The novel itself, we should remember, makes the influence of individual perception on our access to reality and truth a predominant theme. One of the reasons *Frankenstein* juxtaposes so many different discourses and forms of communication is to emphasize the manner in which psychological states of mind and particular modes of communication and thinking affect characters' views of the world and their own ethical and social responsibilities. To go further in understanding this aspect of the novel's formal features we have to return to the specific fictional genres from which it was born.

FRANKENSTEIN AND THE GOTHIC NOVEL

The generic features of *Frankenstein* (its language, form and style) have always provided its readers with a series of important questions. *Frankenstein* is, as most people who begin to read it already know, a Gothic novel: it features prominently in many of the currently available academic studies of Gothic fiction. Shelley highlights the Gothic features of her work in the 1831 Introduction. Describing the famous ghost story competition entered into by Byron, his personal physician Dr Polidori, P. B. Shelley and herself, in Byron's Via Diodati, on the banks of Lake Geneva, in the summer of 1816, she writes:

> I busied myself *to think of a story*, – a story to rival those which had excited us to this task. One which would speak to the mysterious fears of our nature, and awaken thrilling horror – one to make the reader dread to look round, to curdle the blood, and quicken the beatings of the heart. (B, pp. 355–6)

There are in fact no 'ghosts' in *Frankenstein*, but readers of the 1831 Introduction understand that Shelley is positioning her text within the field of Gothic fiction, which gained popularity in the eighteenth century and continued its mass appeal throughout the nineteenth century. Shelley is, in her account of her novel's origin, exploiting important generic distinctions operative in early nineteenth-century literature. Her account of her objective in thinking of a story appears to relate her novel to a class of fiction (Gothic) which has for its prime motive the generation of pleasure through the exploitation of fear, suspense and horror. The assumption appears to be that as a Gothic novel *Frankenstein*'s intent upon the reader is to provide pleasure rather than to instruct or to affect (influence) public opinion on important socio-political issues of the day. This is an assumption which works only if we view the genre of Gothic fiction as being essentially apolitical, a mode of novel writing outside of ideological conflicts and debates. Such an understanding of Gothic literature is, as most critics would now agree, fundamentally untenable. The Gothic novel played an important and diverse part in 'the war of ideas' during and beyond the Romantic period.

In understanding *Frankenstein*'s relation to the Gothic novel, we have to remind ourselves of how Shelley's earliest readers (in particular her reviewers) classified her novel. When we return to *Frankenstein*'s earliest reviews we see that the novel was received as another example of what many call 'the Godwinian novel'. The *Edinburgh Magazine* reviewer, for example, states: 'It is formed on the Godwinian manner, and has all the faults, but many likewise of the beauties of that model' (B, p. 306). John Wilson Croker's antagonistic review in the *Quarterly Review* goes further: 'Our readers will guess . . . what a tissue of horrible and disgusting absurdity this work presents. – It is piously dedicated to Mr. Godwin, and is written in the spirit of his school' (B, p. 308). We will look again at these reviews in Chapter 4, but for now they are sufficient to alert us to the fact that *Frankenstein*'s first generic classification was not as a pure Gothic novel but rather as an example of the kind of novel associated with her father. What is a Godwinian or, as it was often called, a 'Jacobin' novel, and how does *Frankenstein* relate to it?

In his review in *Blackwood's Edinburgh Magazine*, Walter Scott shows himself subtly aware of the distinction between 'romances' which simply revel in the 'marvellous' and the 'supernatural', solely intent on 'pampering the imagination with wonders' (B, pp. 300, 301) and those novels which employ such devices for 'the purpose of political satire, and sometimes to the general illustration of the powers and workings of the human mind' (B, p. 303). In this later category of 'romance' novel, Scott lists Swift, Bergerac and Godwin, naming the latter's *St Leon* (1799) as an exemplary instance, before adding: 'Frankenstein is a novel upon the same plan with Saint Leon; it is said to be written by Mr Percy Bysshe Shelley, who, if we are rightly informed, is son-in-law to Mr Godwin; and it is inscribed to that ingenious author' (B, p. 303). Scott here is referring to the novel's dedication to Godwin, but he also had some reason for believing P. B. Shelley to be the author, since it had been P. B. Shelley and not Mary (who wished at this stage to remain anonymous), who had sent *Frankenstein* to Scott (see P. B. Shelley, *Letters*, vol. 1, p. 590). Scott's remarks are important because they warn us against using a too simplistic distinction between fictional 'romance' and the emergent form which would develop into the dominant nineteenth-century realist novel. Scott's remarks remind us that 'romance' fictions are not all of one kind and that while some use imaginative scenarios purely to entertain, other varieties of 'romance' fiction have a clear socio-political intent beneath their exploitation of the fantastic, the implausible and the imaginary. Such a distinction is an important reinforcement of the contemporary identification of *Frankenstein* as a Godwinian novel.

THE GODWINIAN NOVEL

Godwin, like his daughter, produced very different kinds of novels over his six decades of literary authorship. The core features of the Godwinian novel, however, are to be found in Godwin's first two mature fictional productions, *Things As They Are; or The Adventures of Caleb Williams* (first published in 1794) and *St Leon: A Tale of the Sixteenth Century* (first published in 1799). In these two novels, Godwin adopted features of the well-established Gothic novel and turned them on their head. That statement can be demonstrated by juxtaposing a central passage from *Caleb Williams* with a similarly central scene from Jane Austen's *Northanger Abbey*, a novel first published in the same year as *Frankenstein*, 1818, although written much earlier, at the end of the 1790s. Austen's novel brilliantly exploits and plays with the fears created in late eighteenth-century Britain by the rise of the popular novel and the concomitant rise in the reading public, with its taste for romance fictions. Given such a rise in reading during the 1790s, the dominant forces in British society, at war with republican France abroad and with revolutionary and reformist agitation at home, grew steadily nervous at the potential social impact of an emerging mass readership (see Alan Richardson). Whether Austen's novel satirizes or joins in the conservative alarm at novel reading is a question best left to Austen specialists. What is certain is that *Northanger Abbey* stages an anxiety over the influence of reading in its central plot of a young woman, Catherine Morland, an avid reader (we might say consumer) of 'romance' fiction, who becomes so influenced by the novels she reads that she does not adequately learn the ability to distinguish between fiction and reality. Catherine Morland is a 'female Quixote', a figure who is prevalent in many of Mary Shelley's own texts (see Bunnell, Gonda, Moskal, Webster-Garrett). Catherine, as female version of Cervantes's Don Quixote, mistakes the products of her novel-filled imagination with the reality around her, and specifically she comes to the ludicrously unfounded conclusion that the father of her beloved is the murderer of his wife. This is the kind of thing (evil husbands secretly murdering their wives and successfully suppressing the fact) that happens in the romance novels Catherine reads, and so, disastrously (or nearly so), Catherine assumes that this is also what has happened in the lives of those to whom she is attached. When Henry Tilney realizes the delusions his sweetheart has been entertaining he is horrified and quickly redirects her mind towards the reality of the world around her. The language in which Henry performs this necessary act of epistemological realignment is crucial:

> If I understand you rightly, you had formed a surmise of such horror as I have hardly words to – Dear Miss Morland, consider the dreadful nature of the suspicions you have entertained. What have you been judging from? Remember the country and the age in which we live. Remember that we are English, that we are Christians. Consult your own understanding, your own sense of the probable, your own observation of what is passing around you – Does our education prepare us for such atrocities? Do our laws connive at them? Could they be perpetrated without being known, in a country like this, where social and literary intercourse is on such a

footing; where every man is surrounded by a neighbour of voluntary spies, and where roads and newspapers lay everything
open? Dearest Miss Morland, what ideas have you been
admitting? (Austen, p. 172)

The language of Henry's speech is tantalisingly double-edged,
punctuated as it is by 'voluntary spies' and a sense of a nation in
which surveillance is total. However, it is clear that Catherine
must learn the lesson that the realm of romance novels is not
coincidental, is even frequently opposed, to the realm of late
eighteenth-century British social reality. Catherine's confusion
on this point has almost led her to disaster. The world of
romance novels (including the many Gothic novels Catherine
devours) is one which is full of the improbable, the implausible,
and the downright irrational. It is a world full of characters who
express themselves in excessive, hyperbolic language (just as
Catherine has learnt to do); it is not a world which exists to cul-
tivate that most important of all faculties: the faculty of reason.
It is irrational, it would appear, to confuse the world of romance
fiction with that of social reality; it is rational, it would appear,
to keep them very firmly apart, even in opposition.

Godwin's philosophical and political theories, as we saw in
Chapter 1, are based on what must seem a very similar emphasis
on the cardinal importance of the faculty of reason. One would
imagine, therefore, that Godwin would line up alongside Austen in
her apparent downgrading of romance fiction and Gothic novels;
that he would be as cautious as Austen is regarding the influence
on impressionable minds of the kind of fiction which focuses on
the improbable, the implausible and the irrational. The fact of the
matter is, however, that Godwin created his characteristic mode of
fiction out of a blending of realistic with romance (Gothic) forms.
This is dramatically evident in *St Leon*, a novel about a sixteenth-
century man gifted with the philosopher's stone and the *elixir vitae*
(in other words, the secrets of unlimited wealth and immortality).
Caleb Williams also presents us with a novel in which romance is
initially figured in terms of immaturity and even irrationality (it
causes Falkland to embrace outdated notions of chivalry and
Caleb to develop a dangerously irrational curiosity), only for the

novel to develop gradually into a Gothic story of pursuit, escape, imprisonment, improbable powers of domination and increasingly excessive psychological and discursive displays by its central characters. Falkland, for example, begins the novel as a noble, virtuous, respectable and respected man. However, when Caleb expresses his wish to leave his service (having learnt the terrible secret that Falkland murdered the despicable tyrant, Mr Tyrrel), Falkland speaks precisely like a Gothic villain:

> Do not imagine I am afraid of you! I wear an armour, against which all your weapons are impotent. I have dug a pit for you; and, whichever way you move, backward or forward, to the right or to the left, it is ready to swallow you . . . Begone, miscreant! reptile! and cease to content with unsurmountable power! (Godwin, *Novels*, vol. 3, p. 138)

This speech might appear like a piece of pure Gothic fantasy. Its language is excessive, irrational, beyond belief: the rational reader surely must laugh at the idea of a single man possessing 'insurmountable power'. The rest of the novel backs up every word Falkland says, however: he does, in fact, as an aristocratic man, in a contemporary England dominated by the aristocratic class, possess the power to pursue Caleb, the wrongly accused lower-class servant, wherever he goes and whatever disguise he adopts. As far as Caleb (and men like him) is concerned, a man like Falkland does possess 'unsurmountable power'. Gothic language (a language of hyperbole) turns out to be, given things as they are, realistic language in *Caleb Williams*.

The Godwinian novel can be described in various ways (see Butler, *Jane Austen*; Clemit, *Godwinian Novel*; Kelly; Rajan, *Supplement of Reading*). The blending, rather than the separation, of romance and realist forms is one of its principal features, however. It is a feature which demonstrates the manner in which generic forms, styles and language possess an ideological as well as an aesthetic and literary dimension. The human world, *Caleb Williams* demonstrates, should be rational, free from the irrational forces of power, corruption and despotism, free from superstition, bigotry and prejudice, but, unfortunately, it is not.

Godwin agrees with Austen's Henry Tilney that a rational world would be one in which we could separate rational forms from irrational forms (like those present within the narratives of Gothic novels), he disagrees with Tilney when the latter asserts that 1790s England provides us with such a social world. The main title of Godwin's novel is *Things As They Are*, a phrase which was already associated with a mode of radical literature and thought described by its conservative opponents as Jacobin. The Jacobin party was the party of Robespierre in a post-revolutionary France dominated by terror and the guillotine. Things as they are, in the England of 1794, unfortunately, are far closer to the irrationalities displayed in Gothic romance novels than a man like Henry Tilney would ever admit. When Thomas (who certainly earns his Biblical name), once friend of Caleb, now sworn enemy, finally sees Caleb in the prison conditions that Falkland's lies have placed him within, he sums up a realization Godwin hoped to provoke in all his readers:

> Zounds, how I have been deceived! They told me what a fine thing it was to be an Englishman, and about liberty and property, and all that there; and I find it is all a flam. Lord, what fools we be! Things are done under our very noses, and we know nothing of the matter; and a parcel of fellows with grave faces swear to us that such things never happen but in France, and other countries the like of that. Why, you han't been tried, ha you? (Godwin, *Novels*, vol. 3, p. 180)

Thomas's reaction can be usefully compared to the speech of Henry Tilney. While Tilney tries to get Catherine Morland to recognize that in England Gothic abuses of power and inhuman, irrational systems do not exist, Thomas's firsthand experience of the conditions of English prisoners awakens him from the complaisant sense of England as a rational, just system. Tragically, as Thomas realizes, the Gothic novel is a rather appropriate literary vehicle through which to represent 'things as they are' in 1790s England.

The Godwinian novel or Jacobin novel, pioneered by Godwin himself, but also adopted and adapted by Wollstonecraft,

Thomas Bage, Elizabeth Inchbald and others, employs Gothic and romance forms in order to present a realistic picture of contemporary British and European society. As a form, this kind of novel effects an ideological and aesthetic fusion of forms (realism and romance) which are often, erroneously, described as opposing trends in the development of the novel form. When *Frankenstein*'s reviewers styled it Godwinian they had in mind precisely the kind of political reformism associated with *Caleb Williams* and *St Leon*. Criticisms of *Frankenstein*'s 'tissue of horrible and disgusting absurdity', to use Crocker's words, do not simply refer to the novel's Gothic features, they are also a reaction to its implicit political radicalism, its post-Jacobin continuation of 'the spirit' of Godwin's and Wollstonecraft's 'school'. There are other formal features of the Godwinian novel which we need to understand, before we can take this look at form, style and language back into a discussion of *Frankenstein*'s apparent political equivocation.

Scott's review alerts us to an important feature of the Godwinian novel when he refers to authors' use of romance conventions to illustrate 'the powers and workings of the human mind'. In this critical response Scott produces a very fine gloss on the fictional approach of Godwin. An early chapter of the revised versions of *Political Justice* is entitled 'The Characters Of Men Originate In Their External Circumstances' (Godwin, *Political*, vol. 4, p. 16). Godwin rejected religious and metaphysical notions that human beings were born with innate qualities and characters. This rejection of innate ideas, which derives from the rational philosophy of John Locke, was an important part of the rational Enlightenment of the reformist and revolutionary thought of eighteenth-century Europe. In his essay 'Of History and Romance' Godwin suggests that romances (novels) may well be as enlightening (and as truthtelling) as historical narratives, since: 'True history consists in a delineation of consistent, human character, in a display of the manner in which such a character acts under successive circumstances' (Godwin, *Political*, vol. 5, p. 301). If circumstances create human character, then the novelist is in a peculiarly advantageous position in following the manner in which certain characters will inevitably respond to a certain set of circumstances. The novelist of the Godwinian school becomes a kind of scientist of the human being, a mental anatomist, to employ the title of William D. Brewer's study of Godwin's and Shelley's fictional works. A focus on human psychology and how it is affected by external circumstances is a major feature of the Godwinian novel, and once again suggests a deep influence by that fictional form on *Frankenstein*. Following Godwin's fictional explorations of situated and contextualized human character, Shelley's novel asks us at each stage to assess whether each characters' actions and responses are rational, and if not, what has caused each breakdown in reason.

It is typical of the Godwinian novel to present scenarios in which reason breaks down or is not exercised, and to then not only demonstrate the inevitable consequences of such a breakdown in reason but also to place the reader in a situation in which they can imagine acting differently (more rationally). We should be careful here, however, not to extract this one aspect of the Godwinian novel and produce through it oversimplified readings of Godwin's or Shelley's novels. This brings us to a related feature of the Godwinian novel, which again clearly influences *Frankenstein*: the development of truly ambivalent fictional characters. St Leon loses everything he has because of his possession of the philosopher's stone and the *elixir vitae*, but it would be a rather impoverished reading which simply saw him as a flawed character who should have known better and acted differently. St Leon has authentic social plans for his life and the gifts the stranger gives him. For the entirety of the novel the reader has a great deal of sympathy for him. St Leon is no villain. He is, in fact, an ambivalent, flawed man, full of good qualities and equally burdened by serious weaknesses. We can say the same of Falkland and Caleb Williams, and in fact we can say the same of most of Godwin's major fictional characters. The Godwinian novel does not present stock heroes to admire and villains to deplore, it presents radically ambivalent human beings whose stories retain our sympathy at the same time that they challenge our sense of reason and the possibilities for rational action in the social world. Shelley's central characters – Frankenstein, the creature, Walton – all share this Godwinian character of radical ambivalence. They are characters with whom we sympathize and yet they are characters who, each in their own way, demonstrate disastrous lapses in reason and ethical judgement. A reading of *Frankenstein* which quickly writes Victor off as a morally flawed character unworthy of our sympathy is a reading which drastically reduces (to a simplified, black and white moralism) the radical ambiguities explored in the novel. The long history of adapting the novel to the stage and the screen and to cultural debates about science and technology has frequently obscured this simple fact: *Frankenstein* makes little sense as a novel if we read Victor without the sympathy his story deserves.

FRANKENSTEIN AND THE GODWINIAN NOVEL

Like *Caleb Williams* and *St Leon* before it, *Frankenstein* challenges its readers to imagine how rationality might be more successfully established in the world. In this sense it also demonstrates another important feature of the Godwinian novel: its emphasis on the reader's rational judgement. Godwin is rightly credited with directing the socio-politically orientated novel of the eighteenth century away from overtly didactic forms towards a demonstration of 'things as they are' (*showing* rather than *telling*) which places ultimate responsibility for judgement on the reader themselves. This feature of the Godwinian novel is vividly apparent in Wollstonecraft's unfinished novel *The Wrongs of Woman: Or, Maria* (1798). The novel does possess a third-person narrator but, crucially, it is the exchange of autobiographical narratives between two women of different social class which leads them and the reader towards an understanding of the general 'wrongs of woman' in contemporary British society. The first person narratives of *Caleb Williams* and *St Leon* are similar, in that they work to provoke the private judgement of the novels' readers without the use of a didactic, third-person, omniscient narrator. This feature of the Godwinian novel inherited by Shelley is clearly of major importance in understanding *Frankenstein*. The fact that the novel presents the reader with three first-person narrators with no external guide to arbitrate between their frequently contradictory and thoroughly subjective perspectives, generates, as many critics have noted, a novel which places a huge emphasis on the reader's own interpretive responses.

Reading *Frankenstein* in terms of the Godwinian novel brings us back to the question of its ultimate ideological intention and meaning. Godwin and Wollstonecraft, believers in the Enlightenment idea of reason and its capacity to guide human beings towards foundational ethical truths, wrote their novels confident that their readers would respond in calculable ways. When she exhibits, through her female characters, individual narratives of oppression and injustice, Wollstonecraft is confident that her readers (like those characters) will come to understand the general, social 'wrongs of woman'. When in *Caleb Williams*, he presents the narrative of his lower-class protagonist, Godwin is confident that readers will not only see 'things as they are' more clearly, but in that clearer vision will rationally understand the need for social reform. We have spent some time in this chapter establishing the influence upon *Frankenstein* of the Godwinian novel. In terms of its presentation of first-person narratives, its utilization of Gothic forms, its focus on the psychology of individuals, the ethical ambivalence of its main male characters and in many other respects, *Frankenstein* is clearly the product of the novel form Shelley inherited from her father and mother. We cannot, however, be as clear about its socio-political intentions; its openness to strikingly divergent interpretations is a feature which unsettles and complicates any attempt to claim for it the kind of clear reformist agenda promoted by the novels of her parents. We return here to Baldick's reading of the novel's apparent political equivocation. That Shelley intended her novel to be more politically and ethical ambiguous than other examples of the Godwinian novel is suggested by its frame narrative and, in particular, the concluding role that frame plays.

A feature of the Godwinian novel's non-didactic narrative approach is the utilization of scenes of enlightenment and understanding on the part of its characters. After the lower-class Jemima finishes the narration of her own story, the third-person narrator of *The Wrongs of Woman* states: 'Active as love was in the heart of Maria, the story she had just heard made her thoughts take a wider range . . . Thinking of Jemima's peculiar fate and her own, she was led to consider the oppressed state of women, and to lament that she had given birth to a daughter' (Wollstonecraft, *The Wrongs of Woman*, p. 120). This scene of enlightenment implicitly guides the reader towards the interpretation Wollstonecraft desires for her text. Similarly, when Thomas sees for himself the terrible corruption and squalor of the prisoners in an English gaol, the shattering of his previous faith in the justice of English society guides readers of *Caleb Williams* in the direction Godwin wishes them to go. And what of Walton? In many ways the reader's representative within the novel, the first person to hear Victor's narrative, the first person (other than his creator) to hear the creature's story, does Walton undergo a similar scene of enlightenment to those we have noted as generically characteristic of the Godwinian novels of her parents? Does his decision to give up the attempt to reach the North Pole and to return home to the England of his sister, to whom he writes, indicate that the story he has heard has taught him how dangerous it is to so decisively separate himself from the 'feminine' cultural sphere (see Lowe-Evans)? Such a reading might form part of the influential interpretation of the novel which views it as presenting a feminine critique of the culturally male values of scientific and philosophical quest, of heroic male action over and against the claims of a culturally feminine domestic sphere. In this kind of reading, Walton's return indicates to the novel's readers the leading message of the entire novel: that men neglect and marginalize the feminine sphere at their peril and at the cost of a rational and just society. When we read what Walton actually says, however, the decision to return appears far less a transparent gloss on the novel's overall meaning than some of these readings would suggest. Walton complains:

> The die is cast; I have consented to return, if we are not destroyed. Thus are my hopes blasted by cowardice and indecision; I come back ignorant and disappointed. It requires more philosophy than I possess, to bear this injustice with patience. (*1818*, vol. 3, p. 171; see B, p. 237)

These do not sound like the words of a man who has learnt, as the readers must apparently learn, that the culturally male and culturally feminine spheres should be united rather than separated. This decision to return is followed by the last exchanges between the dying Victor and Walton. Surely Victor in those last scenes corrects Walton's irritation and reinforces the novel's implicit message to its readers? Victor's mind, it should be said, is still largely fixed on his own quest, which is to eradicate his murderous creature from the face of the earth. Now dying, Victor has asked Walton to take upon himself this quest. He returns to this theme just before he dies, but in a manner which leaves the reader in great doubt about the justice of such a request:

> When actuated by selfish and vicious motives, I asked you to undertake my unfinished work; and I renew this request now, when I am only induced by reason and virtue. (*1818*, vol. 3, p. 176; see B, p. 239)

Is this a reasonable and virtuous request? Victor continues, but does not help us as readers to form a firm judgement on that question (*1818*, vol. 3, pp. 176–7; see B, p. 239; see Chapter 3, passage 8, below). Victor cannot tell whether his request, which would thwart Walton in his decision to return home, is a just and reasonable one or not. Instead of a clarifying scene of enlightenment, Shelley's novel appears intentionally to place Walton and, crucially, her readers in a position in which judgement is required, but no guidance is to be had. As if to emphasize this, Shelley then allows Victor, in the very last words he utters, first to support but then criticize Walton's decision to relinquish his own quest and return home (*1818*, vol. 3, p. 177; see B, p. 239; See chapter 3, passage 8, below).

Readings of *Frankenstein* which argue that the novel critiques a culturally male tendency to marginalize and even alienate itself from those aspects of society and culture figurable as female are clearly responding to powerful motives and undeniable features of the novel. What is important here, in this analysis of the generic features of *Frankenstein*, is to register how profoundly Shelley avoids indicating to her readers any simple and singular interpretive route. The frame narrative appears to foreground the indeterminacy of the novel, rather than to provide us in Walton with a reader-substitute who can indirectly guide our own interpretation and response.

Generically, as its first reviewers recognized, *Frankenstein* is a Godwinian novel. In subtle and important ways, however, it fosters an indeterminacy of meaning which distinguishes it from earlier versions of that novelistic form. It departs from its Godwinian model in another very important point. *Frankenstein* does not simply employ the formal features of Gothic fiction in order to present an ultimately realist and politically committed vision of 'things as they are', the classic Godwinian novel technique. In *Frankenstein*, the realm of the Gothic and the realm of the 'real' (the established social and representational order) are blended, merged, made to come crashing into each other. Once Frankenstein has made his creature it exists in the realm of the everyday. *Frankenstein*, through this clash of generic forms (realist and Gothic), radically disrupts a series of oppositions upon which human beings tend to establish their sense of reason, logic and order: the rational and the irrational, the real and the fantastic, the plausible and the implausible, fact and fiction, the empirical and experiential against the imaginative and immaterial. In this sense, then, *Frankenstein* can be understood as a novel which takes the Godwinian novel (with its comparative use of realist and Gothic forms) to another level, a level in which the basic oppositions upon which we rely in constructing our sense of order and rationality are disturbed, brought into question. This observation is not one which simply relegates *Frankenstein* back to the idea of apolitical Gothic romances. On the contrary, it indicates a profoundly philosophical as well as political level within Shelley's novel, one which confronts us with the uncanny.

In his account of the uncanny, Sigmund Freud works with (and against) the prior work on the subject by Ernest Jentsch, and he quotes a significant passage from the latter: 'In telling a story, one of the most successful devices for easily creating uncanny effects is to leave the reader in uncertainty whether a particular figure in the story is a human being or an automaton'

(Freud, p. 347). Freud quotes this passage partly because it has within it the major feature of the uncanny he wants to explore: the manner in which the uncanny depends upon a relationship between what is unfamiliar (the strange, the repressed, the other, the unknown) and what is familiar (that which reflects us, asks for our identification, that which is known and of the same order) (see Freud, pp. 345–6; see also Royle). Freud's work on the uncanny is full of examples from literature in which that enigmatic effect is created by the blurring of the normative line between the familiar and the unfamiliar. He writes: 'The imaginative writer has this licence among many others, that he can select his world of representation so that it either coincides with the realities we are familiar with or departs from them in what particulars he pleases. We accept his ruling in every case' (Freud, p. 373). *Frankenstein* is a classic example; with the creature we are confronted with a character who is a monster (*unheimlich*) and yet physically, psychological, emotionally and ethically human (*heimlich*). As David Marshall has noted, the most terrifying and the most uncanny feature of the creature lies not in his dissimilarity or otherness but in the fact that he resembles his creator and all the other humans he encounters (Marshall, p. 208). This is the reason why so much of the drama represented between the creature and those he encounters happens in and around the eyes. The most terrifying feature of the creature resides not in his otherness (ugliness, artificiality, abortiveness) but in his similarity, the familiarity of his form. *Frankenstein* takes the generic features of the Godwinian novel, including its comparative use of Gothic fiction, and develops it to the point where fundamental questions are posed concerning the ethics of human sympathy and thus the political and social ideas available to us. Are we as rational as we would like to believe ourselves to be? What is the limit of our sympathies and modes of identification? Can we bear to acknowledge the monstrousness within ourselves? Can we bear to have that monstrosity reflected back to us? Throughout her prolific literary life, Shelley's work suggests that we can only improve our individual and our social worlds if we ask ourselves these profound and disturbing questions.

STUDY QUESTIONS

1. In this chapter we have looked at the manner in which the Godwinian novel employs Gothic forms to represent 'things as they are' critically. Are there passages in *Frankenstein* which can be said to be using Gothic literature in a similar manner?

2. Because of his position as frame narrator, Walton would appear to represent the kind of reader-substitute frequently made use of in the non-didactic political genre of the Godwinian novel. This chapter has suggested that Walton does not, ultimately, fulfil that role. Through examination of the frame narrative, can you develop that suggestion further?

CHAPTER 3

READING *FRANKENSTEIN*

THE FRAME NARRATIVE OF *FRANKENSTEIN*

Passage 1

I have no friend, Margaret: when I am glowing with the enthusiasm of success, there will be none to participate my joy; if I am assailed by disappointment, no one will endeavour to sustain me in dejection. I shall commit my thoughts to paper, it is true; but that is a poor medium for the communication of feeling. I desire the company of a man who could sympathize with me; whose eyes would reply to mine. You may deem me romantic, my dear sister, but I bitterly feel the want of a friend. I have no one near me, gentle yet courageous, possessed of a cultivated as well as of a capacious mind, whose tastes are like my own, to approve or amend my plans. How would such a friend repair the faults of your poor brother! I am too ardent in execution, and too impatient of difficulties. But it is a still greater evil to me that I am self-educated: for the first fourteen years of my life I ran wild on a common, and read nothing but our uncle Thomas's books of voyages. At that age I became acquainted with the celebrated poets of our own country; but it was only when it had ceased to be in my power to derive its most important benefits from such a conviction, that I perceived the necessity of becoming acquainted with more languages than that of my native country. Now I am twenty-eight, and am in reality more illiterate than many school-boys of fifteen. It is true that I have thought more, and that my day dreams are more extended and magnificent; but they want (as the painters call it) *keeping*; and I greatly need a friend who would have sense enough not to despise me as romantic, and affection enough for me to endeavour to regulate my mind. (*1818*, vol. 1, pp. 11–13; see B, p. 53)

Frankenstein is a novel with a complex narrative structure. It has a frame narrative – we begin and end with Walton, on his failed expedition to reach the North Pole, writing home to his sister, Margaret Walton Saville. *Frankenstein* also employs layered narration, presenting us with the creature's story framed by and contained within Victor's story, which is itself framed by and contained within Walton's epistolary text. This combination of layered and frame narration produces a complex blurring of narrative boundaries. Victor presents to Walton the creature's story; the creature only speaks directly to Walton at the very end of the novel. Victor's story is also presented in a collaborative fashion. We learn near the novel's end that Victor has 'corrected and augmented' the notes Walton has taken while listening to Victor's story. Victor explains to Walton: 'Since you have preserved my narrative . . . I would not that a mutilated one should go down to posterity' (*1818*, vol. 3, p. 157; see B, p. 232). Victor appears concerned about the believability of his narrative. Indeed, Walton remarks that it is 'the strangest tale that ever imagination formed' (*1818*, vol. 3, p. 157; see B, p. 232) and that it was only the physical evidence of the letters of Felix and Safie and sight of the creature that convinced him of its truth (*1818*, vol. 3, p. 156; see B, p. 231; see also Zonana). Victor's anxiety about the narrative he has given to Walton also concerns the motivation behind it, which is very clearly to vindicate his own character. The same can be said of the creature's narrative and his final words to Walton, however. Narrative in *Frankenstein* appears inextricably linked to issues of responsibility and justice. The novel's complexity and openness to interpretation derives, in part, from the fact that Walton, Victor and the creature are unreliable narrators (narrators whose concerns are for self-vindication rather than accuracy or objectivity). Narrative is a weapon in a rhetorical conflict over responsibility and justice in *Frankenstein*. Mutilation – if we take that word as a metaphor for injustice (the mutilation of the truth) – appears to mark all narrative in the novel. Walton is not our ethical guide in *Frankenstein* and, as Clemit states, discussing these issues in relation to the Godwinian novel, its 'multiple first-person narrative seeks to place the reader as true arbiter of political justice in Godwin's manner' (Clemit, *Godwinian Novel*, p. 173). There seems to be something lacking in the act of writing (narrating), as Walton notes, something which requires what Rajan calls 'the supplement of reading'.

The narrative complexities of the novel do not end there, however. This second letter is dated 'Archangel, 28th March, 17—', Walton's first letter is dated 'St. Petersburgh, Dec. 11th, 17—'. Mellor, Crook and Robinson have all discussed the manner in which internal evidence and checking the novel against a perpetual calendar suggests that the frame narrative, as Macdonald and Scherf put it, 'begins at about the date of Shelley's conception and ends thirteen days after her birth (two days after her mother's death)' (B, p. 49). If this is accurate, as it appears to be, then the major events of Victor's narrative, after he goes to the University of Ingolstadt, occur from 1789 (year of the outbreak of revolution in France) into the revolutionary decade of the 1790s (see *Frankenstein Notebooks*, vol. 1, pp. ixv–ixvi). The significance of the 1790s for Victor's animation of his creature is obvious when one remember the revolutionary context of that decade. The fact that Shelley dates the frame around the period of her own conception and gestation is a more tantalizing feature. If we add to that fact a recognition of the link, when reduced to initials, of Walton's sister (who is the silent addressee of the novel) Margaret Walton Saville (MWS) and the author's own initials, Mary Wollstonecraft Shelley (MWS), we cannot help but begin to feel that Shelley is encrypting autobiographical referents into her novel. As Mellor and other feminist critics have suggested, the implication appears to be that Shelley is linking the creation of her novel, what she calls her 'hideous progeny' in the 1831 Introduction, to her own birth and its tragic ('hideous', 'monstrous'?) consequences in the death of her mother.

Apart from these general issues concerning narrative structure, this section of Walton's second letter establishes a number of themes which are developed throughout the novel. It should be noted that even before meeting Victor, Walton's letter establishes many similarities between them, and indeed between those two men and the creature. The letter contains many statements and sentiments which could as easily have come from Victor's pen or the creature's mouth. The most frequently noted similarity concerns Walton's rather compromised expression of isolation. Just as Victor buries himself away in his scientific work in Ingolstadt, only to create a situation of tragic loss and isolation, so Walton's choice of scientific quest creates the situation which he now laments. A feminist reading of this connection between Walton and Victor often bases itself on the assumption that Shelley is highlighting the manner in which male Romantic quest (literary or scientific) separates itself from the domestic sphere culturally figured as feminine. On that basis the irony would concern the fact that Walton laments his lack of friendship and companionship to a person he has chosen to abandon. Noting such an irony would then allow us to recognize how similar Walton's position is to Victor's, and how dissimilar such positions of willed isolation are to the enforced isolation of the creature, a being who desires rather than abandons the feminine. Certain key words appear to back up the relations being drawn between Walton and Victor here, including the word 'enthusiasm' (see passage 3). Practically every reading of *Frankenstein* acknowledges the Gothic double or doppelgänger relationship between Victor and the creature. There is, as this passage illustrates, just as profound a doppelgänger relationship (of reflection, mirroring, uncanny duplication) between Victor and Walton. They recognize this themselves when they meet, and much of the recognition revolves around their shared desire for a friend.

Walton writes to his sister, 'I have no friend', implying as he does so that the kind of friend he wishes for is male, someone like himself. Jacques Derrida, in his *Politics of Friendship*, has explored how that important concept (it forms the basis for the revolutionary idea of fraternity, after all) has, within the philosophical tradition, been conceived in terms of male-to-male relationships, in terms of brotherhood. Reading Derrida on the philosophical tradition of friendship and fraternity, Allen notes how central the issue of education is within it (Allen,

'Unfashioned Creatures'). Walton's expressed desire for a friend backs up that connection, explicitly associating the idea of finding a friend with finding someone who could 'regulate' his mind. Again, these statements create specific links between Walton's expressed lack of an adequate education with later discussions of Victor's own education, and of course ultimately the creature's problematic education by stealth. Just as the creature's desire for a friend can be related to his need for companionship and friendship, so Walton's desire for a friend is intimately connected to his need for educational correction and completion: 'How would such a friend repair the faults of your poor brother!' For Walton and for the creature, Victor appears to be the man who could provide friendship (in the Rousseau-inspired sense of sympathy but also instruction) (see Allen, *Mary Shelley* and 'Godwin, Fénelon and the Disappearing Teacher'). However, passages added in 1831 to an exchange between Victor and Walton on friendship in the fourth letter, encapsulate the reasons why Victor cannot provide what these friendless male figures need. Walton writes:

> I spoke of my desire of finding a friend – of my thirst for a more intimate sympathy with a fellow mind than had ever fallen to my lot; and expressed my conviction that a man could boast of little happiness, who did not enjoy this blessing.
>
> 'I agree with you', replied the stranger; 'we are unfashioned creatures, but half made up, if one wiser, better, dearer than ourselves – such a friend ought to be – do not lend his aid to perfectionate our weak and faulty natures'. (B, p. 319)

As Crook notes, the words of Victor include an echo of Shakespeare's Richard III and his famous physical deformity: 'Deformed, unfinished, sent before my time / Into this breathing world, scarce half made up' (see Crook, *Frankenstein*, p. 187). Allen, in his *Mary Shelley*, has explored the manner in which this Shakespearean image relates, via notions of untimeliness and physical but also rational deformity, to Godwin's figure of the 'abortive man'. According to Godwin human beings must accept (acknowledge, understand, believe) the truth, if it is clearly and successfully communicated to them. He writes in *Political Justice*:

> Man is a rational being. If there be any man, who is incapable of making inferences for himself, or of understanding, when stated in the most explicit terms, the inferences of another, him we consider as an abortive production, and not in strictness belonging to the human species. (Godwin, *Political*, vol. 4, p. 42)

Frankenstein, as we know, is full of misunderstandings, conflicts of interpretations, and ultimately a narrative conflict between creator and creature, along with Walton's clear difficulties in coming to an adequate understanding of the meaning of the stories he has heard. Following the language concerning friendship and education, as it threads its way through the entire narrative, leads us to consider Walton, Victor and the creature as 'unfashioned creatures, but half made up', in that not one of them is in a position to truly enlighten the other.

It would be accurate to describe Walton as desiring sympathy and enlightenment: 'I desire the company of a man who could sympathize with me; whose eyes would reply to mine'. The eyes are traditionally a figure for enlightenment, for that concept which in itself is a metaphor for the arrival within individuals or collective groups of reason, knowledge and truth (all concepts which are figurable through the vehicle of 'light' and sight). The replying eyes Walton desires are eyes which will possess enlightenment and will also gift a greater degree of enlightenment to him. Again, in Walton's letter a major figure is introduced (the eyes, eyesight) which reverberates in hugely complex and significant ways throughout the entirety of the text. When Walton finally comes face to face with the creature he repeats an action (shutting or shielding the eyes from sight) which Victor has performed a number of times in the presence of his creation: 'Never did I behold a vision so horrible as his face, of such loathsome, yet appalling hideousness. I shut my eyes involuntarily, and endeavoured to recollect what were my duties with regard to this destroyer' (*1818*, vol. 3, p. 180; see B, p. 240). Walton and Victor, when confronted by the creature, shut their eyes from what they consider to be a monster, an abortive man. *Frankenstein* makes clear, in subtle and more obvious ways, however, that these men are themselves lacking the insight or enlightenment which would fully open their eyes to the truth of their own 'unfashioned' selves.

THE EDUCATION OF VICTOR FRANKENSTEIN

Passage 2

Natural philosophy is the genius that has regulated my fate; I desire therefore, in this narration, to state those facts which led to my predilection for that science. When I was thirteen years of age, we all went on a party of pleasure to the baths near Thonon: the inclemency of the weather obliged us to remain a day confined to the inn. In this house I chanced to find a volume of the works of Cornelius Agrippa. I opened it with apathy; the theory which he attempts to demonstrate, and the wonderful facts which he relates, soon changed this feeling into enthusiasm. A new light seemed to dawn upon my mind; and, bounding with joy, I communicated my discovery to my father. I cannot help remarking here the many opportunities instructors possess of directing the attention of their pupils to useful knowledge, which they utterly neglect. My father looked carelessly at the title-page of my book, and said, 'Ah! Cornelius Agrippa! My dear Victor, do not waste your time upon this; it is sad trash.'

If, instead of this remark, my father had taken the pains to explain to me, that the principles of Agrippa had been entirely exploded, and that a modern system of science had been introduced, which possessed much greater powers than the ancient, because the powers of the latter were chimerical, while those of the former were real and practical; under such circumstances, I should certainly have thrown Agrippa aside, and, with my imagination warmed as it was, should probably have applied myself to the more rational theory of chemistry which has resulted from modern discoveries. It is even possible, that the train of my ideas would never have received the fatal impulse that led to my ruin. But the cursory glance my father had taken of my volume by no means assured me that he was acquainted with its contents; and I continued to read with the greatest avidity. (*1818*, vol. 1, Chapter 1, pp. 51–3; see B, pp. 67–8)

Victor, at the beginning of his narrative, spends a good deal of time describing the equality and the friendship enjoyed within the Frankenstein household. Chapter 1 in *1818* ends with a reassertion of this scene of domestic equality and happiness:

Such was our domestic circle, from which care and pain seemed for ever banished. My father directed our studies, and my mother partook of our enjoyments. Neither of us possessed the slightest pre-eminence over the other; the voice of command was never heard amongst us; but mutual affection engaged us all to comply with and obey the slightest desire of each other. (*1818*, vol. 1, p. 60; see B, p. 71)

As we are informed at the very beginning of Victor's narrative, the Frankenstein family is an eminent one in Geneva, a city whose most famous eighteenth-century inhabitant was the philosopher Jean-Jacques Rousseau: 'I am by birth a Genevese' Victor begins, 'and my family is one of the most distinguished of that republic' (*1818*, vol. 1, p. 39; see B, p. 63). The connection with Rousseau seems to be intensified by Victor's description of the domestic equality of the Frankenstein household. Rousseau's educational theories, articulated most significantly in his *Émile* (1762), can be said to have presented one of the first child-centred pedagogical theories, an approach to education in which the authoritarian figure of the instructor or teacher is replaced by a teacher who acts as a guide and a friend. This was an approach to education which Shelley's father had strenuously pursued, even to the extent of criticizing Rousseau for not going far enough in arguing for teaching as friendship (see Allen, *Mary Shelley*). Something, however, is going seriously wrong in the education of Victor in this passage, to the point where Victor feels the need to assert a general critique of education as it is currently conducted: 'I cannot help remarking here the many opportunities instructors possess of directing the attention of their pupils to useful knowledge, which they utterly neglect.' The link with Passage 1 appears obvious here, as does the fact that Victor will eventually be guilty of precisely the same kind of neglect of his own creation. Are we to applaud Victor's father for his egalitarian household or are we to criticize him for failing to provide sufficient guidance and instruction to his son?

Shelley made a number of significant and extended changes to the first two chapters of her novel, turning Chapter 1 of *1818*, for example, into two chapters in *1831*. She noted in the Thomas copy she left in Italy in 1823: 'If there were ever to be another edition of this book, I should re-write these two first chapters. The incidents are tame and ill arranged – the language sometimes childish. – They are unworthy of the rest of the . . . narration' (Crook, *Frankenstein*, p. 34). One change was to resolve a contradiction between Victor's statement that his 'family was unscientific', by having a visitor rather than Victor's father explain the 'laws of electricity' and by stating explicitly 'My father was not scientific' (B, p. 326). *1831* cannot be said to resolve the tension within the account of the father's education of Victor, however, since while increasing his lack of guidance in this way, it also reinforces the happy egalitarian nature of the Frankenstein family:

> No human being could have passed a happier childhood than myself. My parents were possessed by the very spirit of kindness and indulgence. We felt that they were not the tyrants to rule our lot according to their caprice, but the agents and creators of all the many delights which we enjoyed. When I mingled with other families, I distinctly discerned how peculiarly fortunate my lot was, and gratitude assisted the development of filial love. (B, p. 324)

1831 in fact reinforces the central point *Frankenstein* makes about the enlightenment theories of education promoted by Rousseau and by Shelley's own father. Frankenstein's parents are right not to tyrannize their children; they are right to be friends rather than authoritarian and dictatorial masters. Such an approach, however, is no guarantee that things will necessarily go right. There is, for Shelley, no guarantee in enlightenment theories and ideas, however desirable and rational they may be. What gets in the way of the enlightenment education of Victor is his enthusiasm, a word which as before with reference to Walton, appears to imply the presence of irrational and uncontrollable elements in Victor's personality. Shelley is very careful with her wording of the sentence that succeeds his account of reading Cornelius Agrippa for the first time: 'A new light seemed to dawn upon my mind.' Enthusiasm here produces something that looks like enlightenment but in actual fact is not. The whole scene is reminiscent and clearly influenced by Caleb Williams' early reading of adventure stories and books of romance, reading material which inspires within Godwin's character the fatal flaw of curiosity.

The distinction between the modern science of chemistry and the antiquated alchemical myths surrounding Cornelius Agrippa is less important than the fact that Victor is at an impressionable age fired with an enthusiasm to break through the boundaries between science and nature. Cornelius Agrippa (1486–1535) was a figure associated with alchemy, the same quest for the philosopher's stone and the *elixir vitae* which had ruined the life of Godwin's Reginald St Leon. Just as Godwin's novel *St Leon* explores the relationship between Necessity and individual free will, so the concept which in this passage appears to accompany and support the idea of enthusiasm is that of fate. The section opens with the idea of Victor's 'fate' (the word 'genius' in that sentence referring to the idea of an attendant spirit allotted to each person at their birth) and it closes with the 'fatal impulse that led to my ruin'. The critics who have argued that the 1831 version of *Frankenstein* softens the political radicalism of the novel have frequently asserted that the changes made by Shelley in that latter version accentuate the idea of fate over Victor's free will. In the ending she added to the revised second chapter of *1831*, for example, Shelley describes the manner in which Victor's instruction (by the visitor) about the 'laws of electricity' made him drop his former studies 'as a deformed and abortive creation' and take up mathematics. He reflects on this incident:

> Thus strangely are our souls constructed, and by such slight ligaments are we bound to prosperity or ruin. When I look

back, it seems to me as if this almost miraculous change of inclination and will was the immediate suggestion of the guardian angel of my life – the last effort made by the spirit of preservation to avert the storm that was even then hanging in the stars, and ready to envelope me . . . It was a strong effort of the spirit of good; but it was ineffectual. Destiny was too potent, and her immutable laws had decreed my utter and terrible destruction. (B, p. 327)

This may seem to increase the 'fatalism' of the 1831 *Frankenstein*, but we should remember that Victor is hardly a reliable narrator, that his words are not to be treated as the words of Shelley herself, and that the idea of fate and the guardian spirit or angel are present already in the 1818 version. What Victor's recourse to the language of fate and destiny does is to foreground (in a language which at the same time somewhat excuses his own actions) the juxtaposition between the enlightenment family environment in which Victor is raised and taught and the 'slight ligaments' (the incalculable and unpredictable) accidents of chance and random occurrence which, as Shelley argued throughout her writing life, will never be eradicated by philosophical systems and the Enlightenment ideas of Necessity and perfectibility.

VICTOR FRANKENSTEIN AND THE IDEA OF CREATION

Passage 3

No one can conceive the variety of feelings which bore me onwards, like a hurricane, in the first enthusiasm of success. Life and death appeared to me ideal bounds, which I should first break through, and pour a torrent of light into our dark world. A new species would bless me as its creator and source; many happy and excellent natures would owe their being to me. No father could claim the gratitude of his child so completely as I should deserve theirs. Pursuing these reflections, I thought, that if I could bestow animation upon lifeless matter, I might in process of time (although I now found it impossible) renew life where death had apparently devoted the body to corruption.

These thoughts supported my spirits, while I pursued my undertaking with unremitting ardour. My cheek had grown pale with study, and my person had become emaciated with confinement. Sometimes, on the very brink of certainty, I failed; yet still I clung to the hope which the next day or the next hour might realize. One secret which I alone possessed was the hope to which I had dedicated myself; and the moon gazed on my midnight labours, while, with unrelaxed and breathless eagerness, I pursued nature to her hiding places. Who shall conceive the horrors of my secret toil, as I dabbled among the unhallowed damps of the grave, or tortured the living animal to animate the lifeless clay? My limbs now tremble, and my eyes swim with the remembrance; but then a resistless, and almost frantic impulse, urged me forward; I seemed to have lost all soul or sensation but for this one pursuit. It was indeed but a passing trance, that only made me feel with renewed acuteness so soon as, the unnatural stimulus ceasing to operate, I had returned to my old habits. I collected bones from charnel houses; and disturbed, with profane fingers, the tremendous secrets of the human frame. In a solitary chamber, or rather cell, at the top of the house, and separated from all the other apartments by a gallery and staircase, I kept my workshop of filthy creation; my eyeballs were starting from their sockets in attending to the details of my employment. The dissecting room and the slaughter-house furnished many of my materials; and often did my human nature turn with loathing from my occupation, whilst, still urged on by an eagerness which perpetually increased, I brought my work near to a conclusion. (*1818*, vol. 1, Chapter 3, pp. 89–92; see B, pp. 81–3)

This is one of the most critically discussed passages in the novel. Alone in his laboratory, cut off from human society, Victor works with the dead bodies of humans (gleaned from the dissecting room) and dead animals (the slaughter-house) in order to conquer the secrets of animation and to create a 'new species'. The scene is dominated by the nature of Victor's enthusiasm, which has now become a 'hurricane' that carries him along in his attempt to break through previously impenetrable barriers. The scene is full of the tension that such a breakthrough excites and is of course loaded with religious connotations. To create life is the traditional privilege of God, and as he nears that ability

Victor uses a godlike language which clearly indicates how close to the border between sanity and insanity, rationality and irrationality he has moved. The religious language of creation and animation in the first paragraph also relates to the themes of education and enlightenment we have established in the previous passages. Victor wants to 'pour a torrent of light into our dark world', although we cannot perhaps help but notice, in his midnight labours and his 'workshop of filthy creation', that his 'world' is somewhat 'darker' than it need be. His desire to 'bestow animation upon lifeless matter' echoes Godwin's descriptions of the education of young children in his 1797 book *The Enquirer*: 'When a child is born, one of the earliest purposes of his institutor ought to be, to awaken his mind, to breathe a soul into the, as yet, unformed mass' (Godwin, *Political*, vol. 5, p. 84). 'The pupil', Godwin states elsewhere in the same text, 'is the clay in the hands of the artificer' (Godwin, *Political*, vol. 5, p. 113). Animation, as a concept concerned with education and enlightenment, gives us the teacher as a kind of Promethean figure (creating human beings out of clay), but it also, as Allen has demonstrated, contains its own contradictions, since in Godwin's Enlightenment terms reason cannot be given to a person but is to be understood as a universal feature of human nature. Each human being has the faculty of 'private judgement' or reason within themselves, and the task of education is to encourage the exercise of that inherent attribute. It is, in other words, unreasonable to argue that one could give the inherent faculty of reason to another.

It is worth pursuing the connection between Godwin's educational theories and the language of this scene, since it allows us to recognize fundamental contradictions in both. Just as Godwin's educational theories can never resolve the tension between education as a kind of Promethean moulding and animation and education as the liberation of a rational faculty already present within each child, so Victor remains blind to the fact that even if he can learn the secrets of animation this is not the same as being in a position to provide happiness and to guarantee 'gratitude' in that animated other. In the very quest to gain the ability to animate, even create, an other being or even a 'species' of other beings, Victor is forgetting the *otherness* (which includes the unpredictability) of those beings. In the image of himself as a father, Victor appears to have forgotten the inability of fathers to guarantee happiness in their children.

The play of light and dark in the passage deepens our sense of its ironic oppositions and contradictions. Victor's desire is to bring enlightenment into the world, and yet his work seems perilously close to 'black magic'; his aim is to create a 'new species' of 'happy and excellent natures' and yet his materials are dead, filthy and repulsive; he is driven compulsively on in his work, although his 'human nature' turns 'with loathing' at that same project; his aim is to create life, yet this plunges him into the 'unhallowed' world of the dead and into forms of work he describes as 'torture'; his desire is to create beauty, yet his work turns his own cheek pale and harms his own body. In his quest to create life, of course, Victor will ultimately help to destroy not only his own but those of his family, friends and the very being he creates.

Enthusiasm is an ambivalent word in Shelley's novel. Indicating Victor's desire to add to knowledge and create happiness in others, it also clearly works to indicate blindness to the reality of his actions and situation. Victor appears a radically ambivalent figure, a man who combines insight and blindness, enlightenment and obsessive desire. Again, these underlying themes appear to be intensified by images of light and sight. The moonlight that discovers (illuminates) Victor's pursuit of nature's 'hiding places' will return in the animation scene in the next chapter (vol. 1, Chapter 4) and in the scene of Elizabeth's death, as 'on seeing the pale yellow light of the moon illuminate' their marriage bed he catches sight 'at the open window' of 'a figure the most hideous and abhorred' (*1818*, vol. 3, p. 121; see B, p. 218). Victor's eyes, which during his work 'were starting from their sockets' and yet, in remembering this period, now 'swim', also look forward to the swimming, yellow eyes of his newly animated creature in the next chapter. Victor, a man of science and insight, an enlightened man, does not appear to be able to see the reality of his work, the contradictions it involves, his own divided and ambivalent motivations and desires or the possible consequences of its success. The swimming eyes with which he narrates this scene suggest that he remains, at the end of his life, unable to see 'things as they are'. They also suggest the creature's successful revenge, in that Victor narrates his life story with the 'watery eyes' the creature was destined to possess from his origin.

VICTOR FRANKENSTEIN AND THE REALITY OF CREATION

Passage 4

Unable to endure the aspect of the being I had created, I rushed out of the room, and continued a long time traversing my bed-chamber, unable to compose my mind to sleep. At length lassitude suc-ceeded to the tumult I had before endured; and I threw myself on the bed in my clothes, endeavouring to seek a few moments of for-getfulness. But it was in vain: I slept indeed, but I was disturbed by the wildest dreams. I thought I saw Elizabeth, in the bloom of health, walking in the streets of Ingolstadt. Delighted and surprised, I embraced her; but as I imprinted the first kiss on her lips, they became livid with the hue of death; her features appeared to change, and I thought that I held the corpse of my dead mother in my arms; a shroud enveloped her form, and I saw the grave-worms crawling in the folds of the flannel. I started from my sleep with horror; a cold dew covered my forehead, my teeth chattered, and every limb became convulsed; when, by the dim and yellow light of the moon, as it forced its way through the window-shutters, I beheld the wretch – the miserable monster whom I had created. He held up the curtain of the bed; and his eyes, if eyes they may be called, were fixed on me. His jaws opened, and he muttered some inarticulate sounds, while a grin wrinkled his cheeks. He might have spoken, but I did not hear; one hand was stretched out, seemingly to detain me, but I escaped, and rushed down stairs. I took refuse in the court-yard belonging to the house which I inhabited; where I remained during the rest of the night, walking up and down in the greatest agitation, listening attentively, catching and fearing each sound as if it were to announce the approach of the demoniacal corpse to which I had so miserably given life.

> Oh! no mortal could support the horror of that countenance. A mummy again endued with animation could not be so hideous as that wretch. I had gazed on him while unfinished; he was ugly then; but when those muscles and joints were rendered capable of motion, it became a thing such as even Dante could not have conceived. (*1818*, vol. 1, Chapter 4, pp. 99–101; see B, pp. 85–6)

This passage continues the third paragraph of the fourth chapter of the novel in which the creature is animated. Robinson has argued that this chapter, beginning 'It was on a dreary night of November, that I accomplished my toils' was the opening of the original, now lost version of the story (the Ur-text) which Shelley wrote as a response to the ghost story writing idea in the Via Diodati in 1816 (*Frankenstein Notebooks*, vol. 1, pp. lx–lxii). The previous two paragraphs centre on a description of Victor's initial horror at the creature's appearance:

> . . . I had selected his features as beautiful. Beautiful! – Great God! His yellow skin scarcely covered the work of muscles and arteries beneath; his hair was of a lustrous black, and flowing; his teeth of a pearly whiteness; but these luxuriances only formed a more horrid contrast with his watery eyes, that seemed almost of the same colour as the dun white sockets in which they were set, his shrivelled complexion, and straight black lips. (*1818*, vol. 1, p. 98; see B, p. 85)

The description seems to intensify the series of oppositions and contradictions we looked at in Passage 3. The creature's 'lustrous black' hair and 'pearly' white teeth are offset by his 'watery eyes' his 'shrivelled complexion, and straight black lips'. The emphasis here, however, is less on an accurate description of the creature (is it really possible to visualize the creature from this description?) than on Victor's horrified reduction of his creation to its apparently inorganic parts. Victor here clearly cannot see the creature as a whole being, but responds only to its disconnected elements. The next passage gives us Victor's physical and psychological response to his creature, or perhaps to his own initial reaction. It is notable that in this famous passage Victor flees from the sight of his creature twice. The novel, via Walton's and Victor's quest for scientific knowledge, has already firmly established the theme of men who abandon their families and loved ones. Victor here does not begin his career of disastrous abandonment; he has already begun that career in order to pursue his research. He abandons his family, only for William and Justine Moritz to lose their lives. He abandons his friend, Henry Clerval, only for him to suffer the same fate. Eventually (see Passage 8) he goes to confront his 'adversary' on his wedding night, allowing the creature the opportunity to murder Elizabeth. Godwin's aristocratic Falkland, in _Caleb Williams_, has an uncanny habit of turning up just at the moment of crisis; Victor Frankenstein appears to have a mirror (reversing) uncanny ability to walk or run away at precisely the wrong moment.

Before his second abandonment of the creature, Victor describes what he calls 'the miserable monster' once again. The remarkable thing about this description is its empirical uncertainty: does the creature have a grin wrinkling his cheek, or is that simply Victor's traumatized reading of what he sees? One could ask how Victor could imagine that '[h]e might have spoken', given that the creature has just been animated and has no language. Once again the emphasis is on Victor's perception of the creature rather than the reality of the scene itself. Does the creature try to detain Victor, or is that just another interpretation by Victor of what he perceives? Finally, what does Victor mean by stating 'his eyes, if eyes they may be called, were fixed on me'? Either the creature has eyes or does not have eyes, we might object. But clearly, as we have already noted, the figure of eyes and eyesight work in profound ways throughout the novel, and Victor's uncertainty concerns whether the creature's eyes are in any way enlightened, whether they are fully animated in the sense of demonstrating authentic being. Does this creature possess the inherent faculty of reason, that faculty which alone can animate the eye and give beings insight?

Victor, at the beginning of the fourth chapter, begins that process of naming his creature which continues until his death on board Walton's ship. He calls him 'the demoniacal corpse', a 'miserable monster', a 'being', 'the wretch', and in the last paragraph compares him to a 'mummy again endued with animation', before calling him 'a thing' which 'even Dante could not have conceived'. The last statement is remarkable and often overlooked. Dante Alighieri (1265–1327) was the author of *The Divine Comedy*. The first part of that poem, the *Inferno*, contains the most complete and horrifying account of hell in Western literature. Shelley, at the age of 19, is stating that her literary creation is more profoundly disturbing than the canonical account of hell and all its deformities, horrors and monstrosities. The statement pinpoints, in astonishingly confident terms, the novelty of the creature's status as living being and as inorganic, nonnatural production. Shelley's 'monster' is something new in world literature, a being which disturbs the very categories by which we make logical sense of the world: reality and fantasy, being and non-being, life and death, natural and constructed, organic and artificial, animate and inanimate. Victor will continue to produce a series of nominations for his creature (including 'fiend', 'abortion', 'dæmon', 'spectre', 'vampire', 'devil', 'vile insect', 'detested form' and so on) because, as Shelley well knew, there are no authentic names for a being who questions the very logical categories created by human language. After attending a performance of Richard Brinsley Peake's *Presumption; or, The Fate of Frankenstein*, and noticing that for the creature the play bill had simply produced a dash, she wrote: 'this nameless mode of naming the un{n}ameable is rather good' (Mary Shelley, *Letters*, vol. 1, p. 378). The creature is 'unnameable' because it does not appear to fit with the logical constructions by which we order the world, so that its eyes, for example, may or may not be eyes in the human and spiritual sense. There is an uncanny, radically disturbing possibility that the creature's eyes are *just eyes*, lacking that metaphorical connection to enlightenment and insight that would make them *organs of comprehension*.

The image of the creature's eyes can blind us, however, to the fact that the eyes which are of most importance in this passage are those of Victor. The whole scene is conveyed through his disturbed, traumatized perception and his interpretation of what he perceives. Nowhere is this more apparent than in his famous dream in between his initial encounters with the creature. The dream has been much discussed by critics reading *Frankenstein* from feminist, psychoanalytical and biographical perspectives. In many respects these interpretations can be summarized by Mellor's statement: '. . . *Frankenstein* is a book about what happens when a man tries to have a baby without a woman' (Mellor, *Mary Shelley*, p. 40). The problem with many of these readings is that they too quickly reassert the very logical oppositions the scene disturbs (natural and constructed, animate and inanimate) in order to read the novel through the logical and apparently natural oppositions of male and female, parent and child. The following statements by Mellor are not only somewhat ludicrous as a reading of the scene we are dealing with, they also eradicate all sense of the uncertain, unreliable first-person narrative perception through which the scene is presented to us:

> . . . rather than clasping his newborn child to his breast in a nurturing maternal gesture, [Victor] rushes out of the room, repulsed by the abnormality of his creation. And when his child follows him to his bedroom, uttering inarticulate sounds of desire and affection, smiling at him, reaching out to embrace him, Victor Frankenstein again flees in horror, abandoning his child completely. (Mellor, *Mary Shelley*, pp. 41–2)

It is not possible to call the creature (built so preternaturally large and athletic) a child in any uncomplicated way. The creature disturbs the given categories of nature and logic, and so does Victor's dream: mother becomes future wife, health becomes disease and death and the word created ('the miserable monster whom I had created') becomes hugely indeterminate. Has Victor 'created' his dream or has it arrived without his volition? What relation does Victor have to his dream? Shelley knew full well how overdetermined dreams were. Which is to say, they are eminently interpretable but difficult to fix in terms of their meaning; dreams can be said to have *too much meaning*. The dream, as Macdonald and Scherf state, clearly has one of its literary origins in Adam's dream of the creation of Eve in Milton's *Paradise Lost* (1674) Book 8, lines 460–89 (see B, p. 86). It is also clear that a biographically resonant relation between the mother,

Caroline Beaufort, and death is created in the novel. When Victor returns home after the death of William, he looks at the historical portrait of his mother 'in an agony of despair, kneeling by the coffin of her dead father' (*1818*, vol. 1, pp. 151–2; see B, p. 104). In the scene in which the creature murders William, he describes his response to the miniature portrait of Caroline Beaufort:

> . . . I gazed with delight on her dark eyes fringed by deep lashes, and her lovely lips; but presently my rage returned: I remembered that I was for ever deprived of the delights that such beautiful creatures could bestow; and that she whose resemblance I contemplated would, in regarding me, have changed that air of divine benignity to one expressive of disgust and affright. (*1818*, vol. 2, p. 139; see B, p. 167)

It is clear that on the most literal level the creature means 'portrait' by the word 'resemblance'. It is equally clear, however, in the context of the novel's figurative and symbolic patterns, and from the uncanny description of Caroline Beaufort's 'dark eyes', 'deep lashes' and 'lovely lips' (so reminiscent of Victor's description of the creature at the beginning of the fourth chapter) that 'resemblance' here also involves the creature. Metaphorically, the creature in this scene contemplates the 'resemblance' between himself and Victor's dead mother. The crucial thing about the dream (eminently interpretable as it is) is that it establishes the 'resemblance' between Victor and his creation. Just as his creation is a being who disturbs the logical categories by which we order the world, so Victor's dream demonstrates that within him lies a similar blurring and disruption of apparently natural and logical categories, in particular the tendency for love and desire to transform themselves into death and loss. We return here to David Marshall's important assertion that the most horrifying thing about the creature for Victor, and for others, is his 'resemblance' to rather than his difference from human beings. The ultimate disruption in this scene, which will play itself out through the entire novel, is between self and other, human and monster, Victor and his 'miserable' and divided creation.

THE EDUCATION OF THE CREATURE

Passage 5

But *Paradise Lost* excited different and far deeper emotions. I read it, as I had read the other volumes which had fallen into my hands, as a true history. It moved every feeling of wonder and awe, that the picture of an omnipotent God warring with his creatures was capable of exciting. I often referred the several situations, as their similarity struck me, to my own. Like Adam, I was created apparently united by no link to any other being in existence; but his state was far different from mine in every other respect. He had come forth from the hands of God a perfect creature, happy and prosperous, guarded by the especial care of his Creator; he was allowed to converse with, and acquire knowledge from beings of a superior nature: but I was wretched, helpless, and alone. Many times I considered Satan as a fitter emblem of my condition; for often, like him, when I viewed the bliss of my protectors, the bitter gall of envy rose within me.

Another circumstance strengthened and confirmed these feelings. Soon after my arrival in the hovel, I discovered some papers in the pocket of the dress which I had taken from your laboratory. At first I had neglected them; but now that I was able to decypher the characters in which they were written, I began to study them with diligence. It was your journal of the four months that preceded my creation. You minutely described in these papers every step you took in the progress of your work; this history was mingled with accounts of domestic occurrences. You, doubtless, recollect these papers. Here they are. Every thing is related in them which bears reference to my accursed origin; the whole detail of that series of disgusting circumstances which produced it is set in view; the minutest description of my odious and loathsome person is given, in language which painted your own horrors, and rendered mine ineffaceable. I sickened as I read. 'Hateful day when I received life!' I exclaimed in agony. 'Cursed creator! Why did you form a monster so hideous that even you turned from me in disgust? God in pity made man beautiful and alluring, after his own image; but my form is a filthy type of your's, more horrid from its very resemblance. Satan had his companions, fellow-devils, to admire and encourage him; but I am solitary and detested.' *(1818*, vol. 2, Chapter 7, pp. 104–6; see B, pp. 154–5)

The creature's narrative begins in Chapter 3, volume 2, and largely concerns his gradual education about human society and what he calls the 'godlike science' of language (*1818*, vol. 2, p. 58; see B, p. 137). During his time secreted by the side of the De Lacey cottage, he hears Felix read Volney's *Ruins of Empire* to Safie, and then discovers a 'leathern portmanteau' containing Milton's *Paradise Lost*, the first volume of Plutarch's *Parallel Lives* (see B, pp. 26–7) and Goethe's *The Sorrows of Werther* (1774), all of which he proceeds to read. Anne McWhir has argued that these books 'have incompatible views of the nature of power' and that the creature learns from a 'confused curriculum, and an inconsistent reading' (McWhir, p. 83, 79). Fascinating as McWhir's essay on this subject is, I would interpret the creature's reading somewhat differently. It should be noted that the creature's reading practice is explicitly personal: 'As I read . . . I applied much personally to my own feelings and condition' (*1818*, vol. 2, p. 101; see B, p. 153). Like Victor and Walton before him, the creature's reading and narrative practice is based upon a radical subjectivism, books and people are perceived primarily in terms of their relevance to the creature's own feelings and desires. The second point concerns what the creature finds within the books he reads or hears read. He states: 'I found myself similar, yet at the same time strangely unlike the beings concerning whom I read, and to whose conservation I was a listener' (*1818*, vol. 2, p. 101; see B, p. 153). Before looking at the creature's much discussed interpretation of *Paradise Lost*, we must carefully attend to this statement. We saw at the beginning of the first chapter of this study the nature of that similarity and difference. All the books the creature reads speak to him of the divided nature of human beings. He states of his reading of Plutarch:

> I read of men concerned in public affairs governing or massacring their species. I felt the greatest ardour for virtue rise within me, and abhorrence for vice, as far as I understood

the signification of those terms, relative as they were, as I applied them, to pleasure and pain alone. (*1818*, vol. 2, p. 103; see B, p. 154)

The response to Plutarch echoes the earlier response to Volney. As far as the creature can discern, human beings are ambivalent, divided between beauty and deformity, goodness and vice, benevolence and murderous self-interest. The point is crucial, although the creature does not fully understand its implications. The creature's own reading has demonstrated that he is attempting to compare himself to a divided, contradictory, inorganic and less than coherent 'species'. The question readers of the creature's reading could ask, as Allen suggests in *Mary Shelley*, is whether one can actually compare oneself to a 'species' that is not singular, that lacks unity and that is so radically divided. How can someone find themselves 'similar, yet at the same time strangely unlike' beings who are themselves 'similar, yet at the same time strangely unlike' themselves? Human beings, as the creature's reading powerfully demonstrates, do not possess organic unity and are divided within themselves; they resemble the creature, that is to say, in their similarity *and* their difference. These points, which the creature cannot quite grasp, are played out in his reading of Milton's *Paradise Lost*.

The creature, of course, lacks guidance in his interpretation of Milton's epic poem about Satan's fall from Heaven and Adam and Eve's fall from Paradise. He has no friend to guide and complete his own responses, which are all of a comparative nature. He reads the epic as a 'true history' and appears to come to a very Romantic, Promethean interpretation of God as a tyrant king and Satan as the rebellious slave. Such a reading of Milton's epic can be found in texts such as William Blake's *The Marriage of Heaven and Hell* (1790), P. B. Shelley's *Prometheus Unbound* (1820) and Byron's *Manfred* (1817) and *Cain* (1821). He begins by comparing himself to Adam, but then states that Satan appears a 'fitter emblem of my condition'. The problem with the creature's comparative approach to *Paradise Lost* is that it freezes these characters into specific moments of their histories and in so doing presents them as exempla of singular qualities and singular states of being. The creature describes Adam as a 'perfect creature, happy and prosperous, guarded by the especial care of his Creator', and in so doing he forgets Adam and Eve's fall and the curse of original sin upon all their children. He describes himself like Satan, envious of 'the bliss of my protectors', and yet this description of Satan is not only revised by the creature himself at the end of this passage ('Satan had his companions, fellow-devils, to admire and encourage him . . .'), but it also erases previous statements about the De Laceys and the hardships of their impoverished life together. At the beginning of Chapter 4 the creature had announced: 'They were not entirely happy' (*1818*, vol. 2, p. 54; see B, p. 136), and the labour he secretly performs for them is undertaken 'to restore happiness to these deserving people' (*1818*, vol. 2, p. 66; see B, p. 140). The creature's interpretations (of texts, of historical and fictional characters, of the De Laceys) tend to intensify his agonizing sense of singularity, and thus isolation, by transforming the complex histories of others into singular states of being. These interpretations derive, of course, from his sense of his own singularity, something which is only confirmed by the next text he reads.

The evidence of the *Frankenstein Notebooks* suggests that P. B. Shelley made various additions which emphasize the relation between the creature's reading of *Paradise Lost* and his reading of Victor's journal of creation. It is P. B. Shelley who added the phrases 'my accursed origin', 'the whole detail of that series of disgusting circumstances which produced it', 'given, in language which painted your own horrors, and rendered mine ineffaceable', and added the word 'history' to describe Victor's journal account of his work (*Frankenstein Notebooks*, vol. 2, pp. 350–1). We cannot tell whether it was P. B. Shelley or Mary Shelley who added 'but my form is a filthy type of yours, more horrid from its very resemblance', the original line in Mary Shelley's hand reads: 'I am more hateful to the sight than the bitter apples of Hell to the taste' (*Frankenstein Notebooks*, vol. 2, pp. 350–1). What is clear from these additions to the original text, however, is that in their collaborative fashion both Shelleys began to realize how important it was to stress the creature's horror at his difference from but also his similarity to his creator. His creation, in his own reading, mocks the creation of Adam and of man. He is a 'filthy type' of his creator, and so both different from and yet distortedly similar to Victor and all other humans. He is hateful to humankind, so he states, because of his 'very resemblance'. Another change, this time to the 1831 edition, increases this 'reading' of the text by P. B. Shelley and now Mary Shelley alone, by changing the last word 'detested' to the word 'abhorred' (B, p. 341). Allen has demonstrated how the words 'abortion' and 'abhorred' work together in the texts of both *1818* and *1831* to engage subtly with the Godwinian notion of the 'abortive man' (the man or woman incapable of responding rationally to the truth). For Godwin, with his belief in the Enlightenment idea of reason, the image of an 'abortive man' is generated by oppositional logic in which reason exists or does not exist and in which someone is human or somehow not human. Despite creating a series of memorable fictional characters, all of whom can be described as faulty in their reasoning powers, Godwin's thought – and he is hardly alone in this in Western philosophy, literary and science – remained within an oppositional framework which *others* what it cannot endorse or include within its system and method. *Frankenstein*, on the reading I am presenting, is far closer to Byron's recognition of the 'antithetical' nature of human beings. Byron writes of Napoleon in *Childe Harold's Pilgrimage*, Canto Three (1816):

There sunk the greatest, nor the worst of men,
Whose spirit antithetically mixt
One moment of the mightiest, and again
On little objects with like firmness fixt,
Extreme in all things! hadst thou been betwixt,
Thy throne had still been thine, or never been . . .
(36.1–6. Byron, p. 114)

The lines are complex, and yet they are clear enough on the need for a recognition, in Napoleon, in everyone, of the dangers pro-duced by extremism (Glory or Nothing, Victory or Death, and so on) and the need to recognize the human condition as one 'betwixt' extremes, and I would add the extremism of rigid oppositional thinking. Human beings can never successfully attain to the singular states of Glory, Power, Honour or even Reason in Byron, since they are 'antithetically mixt', and contain good and bad, rational and irrational qualities. This is precisely what the creature has discovered in his reading programme; however, the apparent singularity of his situation means that he cannot apply the insight to his own condition and is not in a position to make a bridge towards community with his fellow beings (that 'species' he resembles) even if he did have the insight. It adds greatly to the pathos of the creature's narrative, and to the reader's sympathy with his narrative, that, despite this, that move (reaching out for community, sympathy and understanding) is precisely the next one he attempts. In the paragraph which follows the one we have been discussing, the creature states:

> . . . when I contemplated the virtues of the cottagers, their amiable and benevolent dispositions, I persuaded myself that when they should become acquainted with my admiration of their virtues, they would compassionate me, and overlook my personal deformity. Could they turn from their door one, however monstrous, who solicited their compassion and friendship? (*1818*, vol. 2, p. 107; see B, p. 155)

Old De Lacey does in fact compassionate with the creature, that is until Felix, Agatha and Safie return: 'Who can describe their horror and consternation on beholding me?' (*1818*, vol. 2, p. 119; see B, p. 160). Even Victor, on the Mer de Glace, shielding his eyes from the sight of his creature and listening only to his words, feels it possible to sympathize: 'His words had a strange effect upon me. I compassionated him, and sometimes felt a wish to console him' (*1818*, vol. 2, p. 149; see B, p. 171). The sight of his physical deformity, however, has, as it did with the De Laceys, a different effect: 'but when I looked upon him, when I saw the filthy mass that moved and talked, my heart sickened, and my feelings were altered to those of horror and hatred' (*1818*, vol. 2, p. 149; see B, p. 171). One of P. B. Shelley's greatest contributions to the novel is surely contained in the passage we have been examining. The addition of the clause 'given, in language which painted your own horrors, and rendered mine ineffaceable' sums up so much of the creature's narrative in its final word. The creature's physical deformity, its inorganic material body, is horrifying to all humans needing to believe in the organic, singular condition of humanity. The creature's needs are 'ineffaceable'; they cannot be given a face since they mirror back in physical form the antithetical, divided, ambivalent and heterogeneous nature of human beings. The creature, in other words, physically displays what human society must repress (its own divided, ambivalent, inorganic status). As many have noted, the word 'monster' has various derivations, including the Latin *monstrum* meaning 'demonstration, proof'. A rare use of the word 'monster' concerns the act of exhibiting something wonderful (Oxford English Dictionary). The creature is not the doppelgänger of Victor Frankenstein alone, he mirrors back the whole of the human 'species', and for that he must be treated like a 'monster' and placed in a position of tragic singularity. It is only when that process has shown itself to be inevitable, given 'things as they are', that the creature begins to adopt the part of Milton's avenging Satan: '. . . I, like the arch fiend, bore a hell within me; and, finding myself unsympathized with, wished to tear up the trees, spread havoc and destruction around me, and then to have sat down and enjoyed the ruin' (*1818*, vol. 2, p. 121; see B, p. 161). But we must be careful in our use of *Paradise Lost* in describing the narrative of the creature. Having stated the above, the creature continues, contradictorily, to call the De Laceys 'my protectors', and he continues to waver between hatred of Victor and a desire to find compassion in others. There is no simple, singular, once-and-for-all turn to evil in the creature. Even after the murder of William and the unjust execution of Justine, the creature requests Victor to 'make me happy' by creating for him a female companion. Much of the significance of *Frankenstein* comes down to how we read the ethics of that ultimate request. We cannot read it adequately if we remain ourselves in a rigid oppositional (right or wrong, good or bad, just or unjust) ethical framework; if we remain, that is, clinging to the idea that human beings are capable of ethical and ontological singularity and purity, or that such singularity and purity is the only authentic basis for social action.

VICTOR FRANKENSTEIN AND THE CREATURE

Passage 6

Three years before I was engaged in the same manner, and had created a fiend whose unparalleled barbarity had desolated my heart, and filled it for ever with the bitterest remorse. I was now about to form another being, of whose dispositions I was alike ignorant; she might become ten thousand times more malignant than her mate, and delight, for its own sake, in murder and wretchedness. He had sworn to quit the neighbourhood of man, and hide himself in deserts; but she had not; and she, who in all probability was to become a thinking and reasoning animal, might refuse to comply with a compact made before her creation. They might even hate each other; the creature who already lived loathed his own deformity, and might he not conceive a greater abhorrence for it when it came before his eyes in the female form? She also might turn with disgust from him to the superior beauty of man; she might quit him, and he be again alone, exasperated by the fresh provocation of being deserted by one of his own species.

Even if they were to leave Europe, and inhabit the deserts of the new world, yet one of the first results of those sympathies for which the dæmon thirsted would be children, and a race of devils would be propagated upon the earth, who might make the very existence of the species of man a condition precarious and full of terror. Had I a right, for my own benefit, to inflict this curse upon everlasting generations? I had before been moved by the sophisms of the being I had created; I had been struck senseless by his fiendish threats: but now, for the first time, the wickedness of my promise burst upon me; I shuddered to think that future ages might curse me as their pest, whose selfishness had not hesitated to buy its own peace at the price perhaps of the existence of the whole human race.

I trembled, and my heart failed within me; when, on looking up, I saw, by the light of the moon, the dæmon at the casement. A ghastly grin wrinkled his lips as he gazed on me, where I sat fulfilling the task which he had allotted to me. Yes, he had followed me in my travels; he had loitered in forests, hid himself in caves, or taken refuse in wide and desert heaths; and he now came to mark my progress, and claim the fulfilment of my promise.

As I looked on him, his countenance expressed the utmost extent of malice and treachery. I thought with a sensation of madness on my promise of creating another like to him, and, trembling with passion, tore to pieces the thing on which I was engaged. The wretch saw me destroy the creature on whose future existence he depended for happiness, and, with a howl of devilish despair and revenge, withdrew. (*1818*, vol. 3, pp. 40–4; see B, pp. 190–1)

Everything Victor states in the first two paragraphs is potentially true. The female creature he is in the process of making might become more 'malignant' than the creature himself. She might consider an agreement made before her own 'birth' not binding. She might come to hate rather than love the creature and leave him even more abjectly alone than before. She might give birth to a 'race' of creatures antagonistic towards human beings, and thus be a kind of anti-Eve, spawning a 'species' of creature at war with humanity. Thus Victor's hypothetical thoughts lead up to the nightmare scenario that the work he is now involved in might be putting the fate of the entire human race in jeopardy.

Everything Victor states here is potentially true. However, none of it is anything other than speculation. Victor, clearly talking himself out of the creation of the female creature, begins to refer to the 'sophisms of the being' he had created. Yet that is not the manner in which he had originally responded to the creature's arguments on the Mer de Glace. Victor there had stated quite clearly how much consideration he had given to the creature's request, and how profoundly the justice and truth of that request had struck him:

I paused some time to reflect on all he had related, and the various arguments which he had employed. I thought of the promise of virtues which he had displayed on the opening of his existence, and the subsequent blight of all kindly feeling by the loathing and scorn which his protectors had manifested towards him. His power and threats were not omitted in my calculations: a creature who could exist in the ice caves of the glaciers, and hide himself from pursuit among the ridges of inaccessible precipices, was a being possessing faculties it would be vain to cope with. After a long pause of reflection, I concluded, that the justice due both to him and my fellow-creatures demanded of me that I should comply with his request. (*1818*, vol. 2, pp. 150–1; see B, p. 172)

Despite the possible danger of the creature, Victor recognizes the justice of his request for a female companion. Now, faced again with the 'filthy creation' of another creature, Victor divides the ethical alignment of that last sentence and places the rights of the creature against those of his 'fellow-creatures', human beings. In doing this he divides his own responsibilities (towards his creature and towards humanity) and positions himself in such a way that a choice (between creating the female or not creating her) becomes unavoidable. He gets to this position, however, through his own 'sophistry': by mounting a series of speculative possibilities and treating them as if they were a solid foundation upon which to calculate his ethical responsibility; by revising the history of his encounter with his creature (instead of referring to the creature's arguments, he begins to refer to his 'fiendish threats'); and by effacing the creature's needs and his responsibility to provide for them and collapsing that aspect of the situation into a notion of his own 'selfish' desire for 'peace'.

Victor presents his decision to destroy his work as the revelation of truth. After he destroys the female creature, he states: 'I had before regarded my promise with a gloomy despair, as a thing that, with whatever consequences, must be fulfilled; but I now felt as if a film had been taken from before my eyes, and that I, for the first time, saw clearly' (*1818*, vol. 3, pp. 54–5; see B, p. 195). That revelation, however, is hugely compromised by Victor's actions: 'The remains of the half-finished creature, whom I had destroyed, lay scattered on the floor, and I almost felt as if I had mangled the living flesh of a human being' (*1818*, vol. 3, pp. 53–4; see B, p. 194). Victor's statements about his eyes allow us to register how profoundly the novel's emphasis on the organs of sight relate to issues of reason and interpretation. If watery or swimming eyes are figures for a lack of reason and enlightenment, for that which is 'unfashioned' or 'half made up', then his eyes are not as reliable here as he believes them to be. We can see this as he sees again his own creation. Once again Victor attributes a 'ghastly grin' to the creature, along with an expression of 'the utmost malice and treachery' upon his face. Once again, in other words, as he had done immediately after the creature's animation, Victor takes his own disgust for an accurate perception and description of the reality of the creature himself. The only description relating to the creature which appears reliable and accurate is the reference to his 'howl', but even there Victor loads the description with pejoratives.

The 'calculations' Victor makes regarding the de-creation of the female creature are deeply flawed and highly subjective, and it is crucial that readers understand this. The fact that Victor convinces himself out of his due responsibility to the happiness of his own creation is clear enough. As a creator, or even simply as a father, Victor cannot wash his hands of responsibility by demonizing the creature and by switching all his sense of moral responsibility towards a generalized notion of humanity. That Shelley may be critiquing Godwin's own arguments about the transcendence of responsibility towards family and individuals in favour of a 'general weal' is suggested by Macdonald and Scherf's inclusion of the relevant passage from the revised edition of *Political Justice* in the appendix to their edition of *Frankenstein*. That is not to say that Victor does not have responsibility towards human society; he does, only he also has responsibility to each individual with whom he is personally connected. Shelley does not believe one can choose between family, friends and general society. She also disagrees with Godwin's Enlightenment belief that human beings can rationally develop what he himself, rather ironically, called 'moral arithmetic' (Godwin, *Political*, vol. 3, p. 73).

The last point is crucial for understanding the manner in which Victor rejects and denies his authentic responsibilities in this passage. Victor's arguments are precisely a kind of 'moral arithmetic' in that they not only attempt to weigh the needs of one individual against the 'general weal'; they are also arguments which seem based on the assumption that Victor can calculate what will happen in the future, how the female creature will behave, how her children might behave, and so on. Victor makes his decision on the basis of a kind of calculation of future events, which as we have already seen are mere speculations derived from the horror of his traumatic return to 'filthy creation'. Part of Shelley's critique of the notion of Necessity concerns her rejection of the idea that the ethical consequences of specific actions can be calculated beforehand. We have already seen how badly wrong his calculations about the happiness of his first creature were (see Passage 3). Godwin states that we can calculate that Fénelon will bring greater benefit to the world than his chambermaid (or valet), Shelley, from the evidence of everything she ever wrote, believes that such calculations are neither human (they go against human sympathy and love) nor accurate. Ethical actions, like those faced by Victor here, are always a gamble. This is something Shelley would have learned, at least in part, from the writings of her mother, especially Wollstonecraft's most influential text, *A Vindication of the Rights of Woman* (1792) which frequently returns to the gamble or wager she believes society needs to make with regard to the treatment of women. One of the most frequently cited passages in Wollstonecraft's text reads, for example:

> It is time to effect a revolution in female manners – time to restore to them their lost dignity – and make them, as part of the human species, labour by reforming themselves to reform the world. It is time to separate unchangeable morals from local manners – If men be demi-gods – why let us serve them! And if the dignity of the female soul be as disputable as that of animals – if their reason does not afford sufficient light to direct their conduct whilst unerring instinct is denied – they are surely of all creatures the most miserable! and, bent beneath the iron hand of destiny, must submit to be a *fair defect* in creation. (Wollstonecraft, *Vindication of the Rights of Woman*, p. 158)

There is a great deal in this famous passage which returns in Shelley's novel and especially the passage we have been studying.

The notion of women being 'a *fair defect* in creation' links to the imagery of 'abortive men', 'unfashioned creatures, but half made-up' and the general issue of whether reason is present, absent, malformed or, as Shelley and Byron would suggest, 'antithetically mixed'. When Victor states that the female creature 'in all probability was to become a thinking and reasoning animal' he seems to be echoing Wollstonecraft's critique of all those male writers and social institutions and practices which deny that women possess the same rational faculty as men, while his hesitation on the matter appears to link him to those men, many of whom, such as Edmund Burke, were alarmed at the prospect of a women gaining the education and socio-political powers previously reserved for men.

The crucial feature of the passage, however – and it is a technique Wollstonecraft relies on throughout the *Vindication of the Rights of Woman* – is the wager over female rationality. Either women are rational and should be treated like equals, she rhetorically suggests, or else they are not and men are right to act like 'demi-gods' and to treat women like slaves. The point that Wollstonecraft's text makes time and again is that it is worth making the gamble, worth wagering on female reason. The implication is clear: if what seems just is wagered on, then we might end up with a more just and equal society. One of Victor's problems, in this context, appears to be that he is unfamiliar with the *Vindication of the Rights of Woman* and its argument, at once ironic and yet profoundly serious, that we must take a risk on justice, that equality and reason must be wagered on.

THE CREATURE'S REVENGE

Passage 7

I had been calm during the day; but so soon as night obscured the shapes of objects, a thousand fears arose in my mind. I was anxious and watchful, while my right hand grasped a pistol which was hidden in my bosom; every sound terrified me; but I resolved that I would sell my life dearly, and not relax the impending conflict until my own life, or that of my adversary, were extinguished.

Elizabeth observed my agitation for some time in timid and fearful silence; at length she said, 'What is it that agitates you, my dear Victor? What is it you fear?'

'Oh! peace, peace, my love,' replied I, 'this night, and all will be safe: but this night is dreadful, very dreadful.'

I passed an hour in this state of mind, when suddenly I reflected how dreadful the combat which I momentarily expected would be to my wife, and I earnestly entreated her to retire, resolving not to join her until I had obtained some knowledge as to the situation of my enemy.

She left me, and I continued some time walking up and down the passages of the house, and inspecting every corner that might afford a retreat to my adversary. But I discovered no trace of him, and was beginning to conjecture that some fortunate chance had intervened to prevent the execution of his menaces; when suddenly I heard a shrill and dreadful scream. It came from the room into which Elizabeth had retired. As I heard it, the whole truth rushed into my mind, my arms dropped, the motion of every muscle and fibre was suspended; I could feel the blood trickling in my veins, and tingling in the extremities of my limbs. This state lasted but for an instant; the scream was repeated, and I rushed into the room.

Great God! why did I not then expire! Why am I here to relate the destruction of the best hope, and the purest creature of earth. She was there, lifeless and inanimate, thrown across the bed, her head hanging down, and her pale and distorted features half covered by her hair. Every where I turn I see the same figure – her bloodless arms and relaxed form flung by the murderer on its bridal bier. Could I behold this, and live? Alas! life is obstinate, and clings closest where it is most hated. For a moment only did I lose recollection; I fainted. (*1818*, vol. 3, pp. 117–20; see B pp. 217–18)

In the angry exchange between the creature and Victor after the decreation scene, the former had declared: 'I go; but remember, I shall be with you on your wedding-night' (*1818*, vol. 3, p. 48; see B, p. 193). It is important to note the wider context of that menacing promise. The creature's entreaties regarding a companion prove to be in vain; he declares, 'You are my creator, but I am your master; – obey!', but Victor will not obey and the creature then spells out what he means by his mastery: 'Are you to be happy, while I grovel in the intensity of my wretchedness? You can blast my other passions; but revenge remains – revenge, henceforth dearer than light or food! I may die; but first you, my tyrant and tormentor, shall curse the sun that gazes on your misery' (*1818*, vol. 3, p. 48; see B, p. 192). The creature continues: 'I will watch with the wiliness of a snake, that I may sting with its venom. Man, you shall repent of the injuries you inflict' (*1818*, vol. 3, p. 48; see B, pp. 192–3). It is then that the creature makes his vow regarding Victor's wedding-night.

It does seem, in this context, somewhat puzzling that Victor remains convinced that he himself will be the target of his 'adversary': 'suddenly I reflected how dreadful the combat which I momentarily expected would be to my wife.' The fact that the creature makes his vow after Victor has destroyed his potential companion ('wife'), that killing Victor would forever deprive the creature of the hope of a companion like himself, and the fact that he could have murdered Victor there and then as they spoke, these pointers to the real target of the creature's revenge appear obvious to the novel's readers. They provide yet another example of the manner in which we have to look beyond the words and the first-person perspective of Victor's narrative. Victor is not seeing things here with clear vision, and his request that Elizabeth retire gives one more example of his tendency to abandon those he would protect. It is useful, in fact, to return to Chapter 5, volume 3, to see just how thoroughly Victor convinces himself that he is the target of the creature's threat and his reflections on his mistake:

Great God! if for one instant I had thought what might be the hellish intention of my fiendish adversary, I would rather have banished myself for ever from my native country, and wandered a friendless outcast over the earth, than have consented to this miserable marriage. But, as if possessed of magic powers, the monster had blinded me to his real intentions; and when I thought that I prepared only my own death, I hastened that of a far dearer victim. (*1818*, vol. 3, pp. 107–8; see B, p. 214)

The fact that Victor blames the creature's 'magic powers' for his blindness to the real intentions behind the vow is another example of how far his demonization of the creature substitutes for any realistic assessment of the situation. Victor's image of himself wandering without a friend over the globe also suggests a total blindness to his own abandoning character. It would appear that whatever he does and whatever he decides he will inevitably abandon Elizabeth. Indeed, feminist and psychoanalytical readings of this scene alert us to the possibility that Victor's real dread is sexual in nature and that his actions on his wedding night can be interpreted as a dread of the female body. Elizabeth's question ('What is it that agitates you . . .?') may well have its ultimate answer in her own body.

These points can be usefully brought into a reading of Victor's first reaction to the sound of Elizabeth's scream. What is the 'whole truth' that rushes into his mind? Is it the truth of the object of the creature's vow of revenge? Is it the full meaning of that revenge? Or is the 'whole truth' something that also encompasses Victor's own self? Does Victor suddenly realize the injustice of his treatment of the creature here? Does he suddenly realize that the creature is somehow connected, on a psychological and ethical level, to his own abandoning personality? Does he suddenly see his own masculine rejection of the feminine in its true form? We cannot know, of course, since Victor's narrative does not answer those questions. The point is, however, that rather like the pause between Elizabeth's two screams, the idea (of Victor's sudden enlightenment and revelation) creates a textual gap, a lacunae, into which the reader is invited to step and within which the reader can explore possibilities. It is another example of the manner in which the novel can generate multiple interpretations through techniques of elision and indeterminacy.

One thing seems reasonably clear: the 'whole truth' is something that involves Elizabeth along with the creature. Just as Victor has erased the creature's authentic needs from his ethical calculations, so he has kept Elizabeth ignorant of the reality of the danger that threatens them, promising to tell her his secret the day after their wedding. The last paragraph brings Elizabeth and the creature together in a scene which dramatically displays and demonstrates the consequences of Victor's actions. It is perhaps significant that Victor describes Elizabeth as 'the purest creature of earth', a phrase which links her to the creature's account of Milton's Adam in Passage 5. The image for Victor appears to be of 'the purest creature' having been murdered by the most corrupt, 'filthy' 'creature of earth'. What Victor does not see, however, is the manner in which the coming together of these two extremes reflects his own lack of responsibility, sympathy and sincerity towards his most significant others. In a rather uncanny but also literal sense, Victor's abandoned child murders his abandoned wife. The scene is the tragic culmination of the history of Victor's unsuccessful struggle with his own nature, his own psychological, ethical and social being. This account is not meant to diminish the tragedy of the actual event (Elizabeth's murder), but it is important even here that we do not forget that we are receiving this scene through Victor's first-person narration. The focus, even here, is still on Victor and his tragic history; the scene is framed by reference to his physical and psychological response ('why did I not then expire!', 'For a moment only did I lose recollection; I fainted').

The scene presented in the last paragraph is also in all probability intertextual in its reference and meaning. As Crook notes, '[t]here is a probable allusion in this death-scene to the woman's pose in Henry Fuseli's *The Nightmare* . . . though it has not been conclusively established that Mary Shelley saw a reproduction' (Crook, *Frankenstein*, p. 150). Fuseli's famous Gothic painting can be found in Mellor's *Mary Shelley* and is used, with variations, in Ken Russell's film *Gothic*. Crook notes that Fuseli's picture is 'vividly described' in Erasmus Darwin's *The Botanic Garden* (1792); Macdonald and Scherf discuss the influence of Darwin on the Shelleys and note how 'Shelley may have known him since childhood, since he was a friend of her father' (B, p. 20). Shelley's connection with Fuseli is often registered through the link between Elizabeth's death scene and Fuseli's painting. In fact, the connections were more profound, since her mother in the first years of the 1790s had 'conceived a personal and ardent affection for him', as Godwin tentatively puts it in his *Memoirs of the Author of A Vindication of the*

Rights of Woman (1798) (Godwin, *Memoirs*, p. 234). A useful discussion of Wollstonecraft's 'strange fixation' on the artist 18 years her senior and unsympathetic to the feminist cause can be found in Lyndall Gordon's biography (Gordon, pp. 174–81; see also Todd, pp. 152–5, 194–8).

Fuseli's *The Nightmare* presents us with a young woman in flowing white nightdress, her head and arms dropping down from the side of her bed, her hair cascading down, her eyes closed, while a horse head peers out (with uncanny eyes) from the dark recesses of the bedroom, and a strange demon (of the size of a young boy) stares not at the woman upon whose stomach he sits, but directly at the viewer of the painting. The effect of the painting is truly uncanny and this effect has much to do with the manner in which the demon figure implicates the viewer into the nightmare scene. When we come to Victor's description, we can immediately see how similar the scene is to Fuseli's famous material representation of the unconscious content of dreams. Of course, in place of Fuseli's demon and horse Shelley has her creature, although he is not visible when Victor describes Elizabeth's dead body. Another change, noted by William Veeder, is perhaps of more significance (Veeder, pp. 192–3). While the face and closed eyes of Fuseli's young woman can be seen clearly. Shelley has 'her head hanging down, and her pale and distorted features half covered by her hair'. The connections created with previous scenes (including the animation and decreation scenes) are multiple and well worth pursuing. However, the abiding significance seems to reside in the covering of Elizabeth's eyes. If her hair did not conceal them, Elizabeth's eyes would now be describable as 'lifeless', 'inanimate', perhaps 'watery'. It is in this, the eradication of comprehension and light from Elizabeth's eyes, that the creature's revenge consists. The revenge is not simply for the de-creation of his own potential female companion, but more profoundly for the continued perception in his creator and all others he has met, of the lack of light and animation in his own eyes. As if to underscore that his revenge has revolved around the issue of sight and insight, the sympathy and understanding eyes can give or refuse to give, light now comes into the terrible scene, the bedroom is illuminated:

The windows of the room had before been darkened; and I felt a kind of panic on seeing the pale yellow light of the moon illuminate the chamber. The shutters had been thrown back; and, with a sensation of horror not to be described, I saw at the open window a figure the most hideous and abhorred. A grin was on the face of the monster; he seemed to jeer, as with his fiendish finger he pointed towards the corpse of my wife. (*1818*, vol. 3, p. 121; see B, pp. 218–19)

For the first time it seems likely that Victor's attribution of a grin on the face of his creature is accurate, and not simply the product of his own horrified projection. It seems likely because of how precisely the creature has reversed the de-creation scene, fulfilled the 'whole truth' of his vow, and placed Victor in the state of being he has, until this point, suffered alone. It is to all of this and more that the creature points.

VICTOR FRANKENSTEIN CONSIDERS HIS ACTIONS

Passage 8

'During these last days I have been occupied in examining my past conduct; nor do I find it blameable. In a fit of enthusiastic madness I created a rational creature, and was bound towards him, to assure, as far as was in my power, his happiness and well-being. This was my duty; but there was another still paramount to that. My duties towards my fellow-creatures had greater claims to my attention, because they included a greater proportion of happiness or misery. Urged by this view, I refused, and I did right in refusing, to create a companion for the first creature. He shewed unparalleled malignity and selfishness, in evil: he destroyed my friends; he devoted to destruction beings who possessed exquisite sensations, happiness, and wisdom; nor do I know where this thirst for vengeance may end. Miserable himself, that he may render no other wretched, he ought to die. The task of his destruction was mine, but I have failed. When actuated by selfish and vicious motives, I asked you to undertake my unfinished work; and I renew this request now, when I am only induced by reason and virtue.

Yet I cannot ask you to renounce your country and friends, to fulfil this task; and now, that you are returning to England, you will have little chance of meeting with him. But the consideration of these points, and the well-balancing of what you may esteem your duties, I leave to you; my judgement and ideas are already disturbed by the near approach of death. I dare not ask you to do what I think right, for I may still be misled by passion.

That he should live to be an instrument of mischief disturbs me; in other respects this hour, when I momentarily expect my release, is the only happy one which I have enjoyed for several years. The forms of the beloved dead flit before me, and I hasten to their arms. Farewell, Walton! Seek happiness in tranquillity, and avoid ambition, even if it be only the apparently innocent one of distinguishing yourself in science and discoveries. Yet why do I say this? I have myself been blasted in these hopes, yet another may succeed.' (*1818*, vol. 3, pp. 175–7; see B, pp. 238–9)

These are the last words Victor says before he dies. They are words which should convince any careful reader of the text that Victor dies still morally confused about his own responsibilities towards the creature he has made and towards his fellow human beings. He begins confidently enough, stating that he finds no blame in his 'past conduct', and yet even that statement is confusing: does it cover all Victor's past actions, including the animation of the creature, or does it relate only to his decision to destroy the female creature and now his original creature? Surely Victor would understand, if he considered things clearly, that if he is right in his quest to destroy the creature he was probably wrong in creating him in the first place. How can Victor find no blame in his 'past conduct'? The rest of the paragraph is an attempt to answer that question, but it is doomed to failure. Victor states that in his scientific work he was under a 'fit of enthusiastic madness' and by doing so offers an excuse for his action. Enthusiasm – a word which has followed us throughout the novel – appears to signify an unwilled alteration in identity. When people are under the influence of enthusiasm, it would seem, they are not themselves, are something other than their rational selves. It is just as important, then, that Victor styles his creature 'rational', something he

had very much doubted during the animation scene and its immediate aftermath. With that rational and ethical recognition on
Victor's part, he then appears capable of admitting his responsibilities towards his creature. This recognition of responsibility,
however, is immediately qualified and quickly erased by the quasi-
utilitarian and Godwinian idea of the greater, 'more paramount'
responsibility of the individual to the 'common weal', or what
Victor here calls 'my fellow-creatures'. He returns, then, in these
lines meant to vindicate his actions at the end of his life, to the
ethical and logical arguments we discussed in terms of the de-
creation scene (Passage 6). We do not need to go over those arguments again; the fact that they end in contradiction (pitting two
completely valid and authentic modes of responsibility against
each other and falsely asserting that a choice must be made for
one over the other) is obvious from everything Victor goes on to
say in this passage.

What is striking in the first paragraph is Victor's reference to
his 'unfinished work'. He makes this reference in the context of
his request that Walton take over his quest to destroy the creature. However, from our careful reading of the figurative patterns
of the novel it is clear that the phrase has a profound reversibil-
ity and overdetermination of meaning within it. The creature
himself was an 'unfinished' piece of work, as of course was his
female companion, but so are Victor and Walton with their
faulty educations and distorted understanding of responsibility.
The fact that Victor has not resolved the tension between responsibility to general society and responsibility to the individual is
made eminently clear in the second paragraph, when he considers the request to Walton. He presents this renewed request as the
product of 'reason and virtue', however it immediately breaks
down into its contradictory parts when he considers its implications for Walton's own life. Victor recognizes that Walton
should not abandon his responsibilities to his family, friends and
country in order to take up the quest to destroy the creature; we
must not forget here, however, that he has also convinced himself
that the creature is a threat to the whole of humanity. Because of
that general threat to humanity, Victor destroyed the female creature. On his own, so Victor's logic runs, the creature is not now a

general threat. All he has said in the first paragraph is that 'I do not know where this thirst for vengeance may end'. Readers will quickly learn from the creature itself that it ends, without any satisfaction or resolution, in the death of Victor. With these considerations in mind we begin to realize that the motives for Victor's actions have changed since he first articulated them in the de-creation scene; he has in fact been the principal agent in creating those changes. Victor's sense of the 'reason and virtue' of his quest collapses as he reiterates it, so that he can only eventually leave the ethical calculation to Walton himself. Victor here recognizes, reasonably enough, that his desire for the creature's death may be dictated by passion and hatred rather than general, ethical principles and objectives. It is important to note that a few pages earlier, Victor had described himself in a Miltonic manner which demonstrates how completely he has been taken over by the dialectical conflict over power, the master–slave struggle for revenge and victory, which the creature (as slave-figure) has instigated through his murderous actions: 'All my speculations and hopes are as nothing; and, like the archangel who aspired to omnipotence, I am chained in an eternal hell' (*1818*, vol. 3, p. 160; see B, p. 233). This focus on the destructive relationship between masters and slaves, a relationship which symbolizes society's domination by systems of power rather than reason and justice, is something Shelley shared with many of her Romantic contemporaries, including her husband, her mother and her father. Godwin's Caleb Williams, on apparently escaping from Falkland's house, announces:

> . . . I thought with unspeakable loathing of those errors, in consequence of which every man is fated to be more or less the tyrant or the slave. I was astonished at the folly of my species, that they did not rise up as one man, and shake off chains so ignominious and misery so insupportable. So far as related to myself, I resolved, and this resolution has never been entirely forgotten by me, to hold myself disengaged from the odious scene, and never fill the part either of the oppressor or the sufferer. (Godwin, *Novels*, vol. 3, p. 140)

This is a worthy and rational determination. Caleb's narration demonstrates that it is also, given 'things as they are', completely unrealizable and unachievable; masters and slaves are locked together in a power play in *Caleb Williams*, a novel which presents a society lacking sufficient reason to halt the repetitious cycle of oppression and enslavement. *Frankenstein* presents a similar socio-political scenario, and like Godwin's novel calls to its readers to see beyond its power-dominated confines. In Shelley's novel, however, our ultimate focus is not on how the master figure maintains his ability to pursue and enslave his victim, but rather on how the creature (unable to liberate himself from a position of alienation and the prison house of social demonization) pulls the master-creator figure down to his own 'hellish' level as a tragic act of revenge. Victor dies unenlightened as to the reality of this scenario, and his last words to Walton betray that lack of insight in their resounding contradictions.

Victor ends by encouraging Walton to find his happiness in domestic and personal relationships with individuals, the very thing Victor failed to do. He then, in complete contradiction, adds: 'Yet why do I say this? I have myself been blasted in these hopes, yet another may succeed'. Not only are these last words in contradiction to the idea of peace and tranquillity and the 'good life' just described, they are divided within themselves. What 'hopes' does Victor refer to here? Does he mean, as the context would suggest, his hopes of catching and putting an end to the life of the creature? There is a doubt, since Victor has just referred to their shared enthusiasm, the dream of 'distinguishing' themselves 'in science and discoveries'. The possibility remains in these lines that, for all the tragedy and agonizing loss his scientific experiments have caused him, Victor is still willing to encourage Walton to face down his mutinous crew and to plough on further into the murderous regions of the Artic. The manner in which Victor's last words suggest an overall moral (unification of the male and female spheres, dangers of an exclusive focus on 'science and discoveries') and yet explicitly undercut that moral, is reminiscent of the ending of Coleridge's 'Rime of the Ancyent Mariner', a text cited by Walton in his second letter (see B, p. 55)

and given even more emphasis in additions Shelley made to the
1831 edition (see B, p. 317). Coleridge's poem ends:

> He went, like one that hath been stunn'd
> And is of sense forlorn:
> A sadder and a wiser man
> He rose the morrow morn. (Coleridge, p. 254).

How one can be 'stunn'd' and 'wiser', or 'forlorn' of 'sense' and
'wiser' is not explained in the poem; it is left to the reader to
ponder such contradictions within the context of the poem as a
whole. Similarly, readers of *Frankenstein* are left with Victor's
contradictory vindication. They are also left with the creature's
final words to Walton, and with Walton's ultimate response to
Victor's narrative and to his meeting with the creature. The task
of seeing the bigger picture, of piecing together the narratives,
perspectives, arguments and counter-arguments presented in the
novel, is left to the reader.

STUDY QUESTIONS

1. Choose one passage from each of the novel's three volumes
   and write a close critical analysis of it, trying to draw out how
   each passage relates to the themes and forms of the novel as a
   whole.
2. The readings of the eight passages extracted from the novel
   have returned frequently to a series of issues and themes
   revolving around eyes, eyesight, light and dark. Can you find
   other passages which develop the kinds of meanings we have
   seen generated from this set of imagery.

CHAPTER 4

CRITICAL RECEPTION, COMPOSITION AND PUBLISHING HISTORY

CONTEMPORARY REVIEWS

The contemporary critical reception of *Frankenstein* provides a significant support for the account of the novel's form presented in Chapter 2 of this study. W. H. Lyles and Jean de Palacio list eight reviews of the novel in the first year of its publication, 1818 (see also Crook, *Frankenstein*, p. xcv). If we look at these reviews, some of them favourable, some of them extremely critical, we see that various shared responses and anxieties are generated within the first readers of Shelley's novel. Schoene-Harwood, in his account of the contemporary reviews, states rightly that they 'fall roughly into two oppositional groups: those quick to voice their moral outrage and indignant disapproval, and those guardedly expressing a sense of intrigue, fascination and respect' (Schoene-Harwood, p. 13). He goes on to at least partly explain this bifurcated ideological response by describing *Frankenstein*'s apparent 'oscillation between scientific fact and individual fantasy', its mixture of 'the prototype of a new literary genre – that of science fiction' and 'the rather worn-out, sensationalist devices of the Gothic novel' (p. 14). In fact, when we look at the contemporary reviews they invariably point to *Frankenstein*'s association with William Godwin and by doing so register the novel's generic and ideological status as a Godwinian novel. The reviewers seem very clear on this point. *Frankenstein*, for them, despite the anonymity of its author, was a Godwinian novel and therefore associated with radical ideas stemming from the revolutionary 1790s, ideas which were still troublingly present in popular fiction and in society, even after the defeat of Napoleonic France in 1815. These reviewers, generally, do not perceive a political equivocation in *Frankenstein*, but rather a direct inheritance of the political reformism and philosophical idealism associated with Godwin himself.

The reviewer in *La Belle Assemblée* states: 'This work . . . is inscribed to Mr. Godwin, who, however he once embraced novel systems, is, we are credibly informed, happily converted to what he once styled ancient prejudices' (see Reiman, vol. 1, p. 44). In order to present a cautious praise of *Frankenstein*, the *Belle Assemblée* reviewer finds it necessary to present Godwin as having rejected the radical views he had expressed in the 1790s. *Frankenstein*, for this reviewer, is inextricably linked with the name of Godwin. When critics wished to criticize *Frankenstein*, they also employed the association with Godwin. In an anonymous *British Critic* review, the author states: 'This is another anomalous story of the same race and family as Mandeville; and, if we are not misinformed, it is intimately connected with that strange performance, by more ties than one' (B, p. 432). The critic goes on to describe the Godwinian school as one which flirts with madness, a common accusation. The review in *The Edinburgh Magazine*, takes a similar, if somewhat more receptive, line, beginning again with the Godwinian connection:

> Here is one of the productions of the modern school in its highest style of caricature and exaggeration. It is formed on the Godwinian manner, and has all the faults, but many likewise of the beauties of that model. In dark and gloomy views of nature and of man, bordering too closely on impiety, – in the most outrageous improbability, – in sacrificing everything to effect, – it even goes beyond its great prototype; but in return, it possesses a similar power of fascination, something of the same mastery in harsh and savage delineations of passion, relieved in like manner by the gentler features of domestic and simple feelings. (B, p. 306)

The review attempts to respond to the combination of fantasy and science in *Frankenstein* by referring to the daily marvels experienced within the age of Napoleon, before once again bringing things back to the novel's Godwinian status:

> We hope yet to have more productions, both from this author and his great model, Mr Godwin; but they would make a great improvement in their writings, if they would rather study the established order of nature as it appears, both in the world of matter and of mind, than continue to revolt our feelings by hazardous innovations in either of these departments. (B, p. 308)

With somewhat grudging respect, then, the reviewer wishes that the Godwinian novelists, one of whom it clearly recognizes in the author of *Frankenstein*, would accommodate themselves more entirely to the known world. The inference is clear: books which refuse to accommodate themselves to the common standards of literary 'realism' are troublingly close to those elements in society which refuse to accommodate themselves to the common standards of political 'realism' and the dominant order. The Godwinian novelists' utilization of Gothic fiction has a perceived potential within it for political radicalism. This idea is the overriding concern of John Wilson Crocker's critique of *Frankenstein* in *The Quarterly Review*. After producing a plot paraphrase meant to emphasize the manner in which *Frankenstein* diverges from the accepted standards of common taste and decency, Crocker states: 'Our readers will guess from this summary, what a tissue of horrible and disgusting absurdity this work presents. – It is piously dedicated to Mr. Godwin, and is written in the spirit of his school'. Crocker warms to his subject, the pernicious and insane (and, the inference is clear, the politically dangerous) Godwinian school, and he continues:

> The dreams of insanity are embodied in the strong and striking language of the insane, and the author, notwithstanding the rationality of his preface, often leaves us in doubt whether he is not as mad as his hero. Mr. Godwin is the patriarch of a literary family, whose chief skill is in delineating the wanderings of the intellect, and which strangely delights in the most

afflicting and humiliating of human miseries. His disciples are a kind of *out-pensioners of Bedlam*, and, like 'Mad Bess' or 'Mad Tom', are occasionally visited with paroxysms of genius and fits of expression, which make sober-minded people wonder and shudder. (B, pp. 308–9)

Crocker's review is not entirely negative. He admits that the author of *Frankenstein* has 'powers both of conception and language, which employed in a happier direction might, perhaps . . . give him a name among those whose writings amuse or amend their fellow-creatures' (B, pp. 309–10). But the connection drawn with the Godwinian school clearly directs Crocker's conservative critical reading and disallows anything but a rejection of its form and its implied politics.

When Shelley's novel was reviewed by her British contemporaries in 1818 it was presented as another example of the Godwinian novel. We can go further, in fact, and note a series of shared responses (whether presented in a positive, a guarded or a negative tone), all of which stem from this initial categorization of *Frankenstein* as Godwinian. It is useful to present these responses in order. The mixing of Gothic and realist forms is viewed by many of the reviewers as a worrying feature of Godwinian fiction. Many of the reviewers also appear anxious about the novel's lack of any clear, guiding moral lesson. That the (then) anonymous author of *Frankenstein* has undoubted literary powers is generally acknowledged, but the novel's popular appeal also appears to make a number of the reviewers anxious. The reviewer in *The Monthly Review*, for example, styles *Frankenstein* as 'An uncouth story, in the taste of the German novelists, trenching in some degree on delicacy, setting probability at defiance, and leading to no conclusion either moral or philosophical' (*Monthly Review*, p. 439). Various reviews appear nervous at the lack of any specifically Christian moral in the novel. As the *Belle Assemblée* reviewer puts it: 'This is a very *bold* fiction; and did not the author, in a short Preface, make a kind of apology, we should almost pronounce it to be *impious*. We hope, however, the writer had the moral in view which we are desirous of drawing from it, that the *presumptive* works of man must be frightful' (Reiman, vol. 1, p. 42). We will return to the word *pre-sumption* in this and the next chapter, but again this response demonstrates a general feeling in *Frankenstein*'s reviewers that the novel requires a moral interpretation in order for its readers to consume it safely. A number of reviewers, in fact, appear anxious about the novel's implicit support for a materialist understanding of natural phenomena. The *Belle Assemblée* reviewer's reference to the 1818 preface, highlights one other common feature of these early responses to *Frankenstein*. The preface to the 1818 edition of the novel was, as we now know, penned by P. B. Shelley. The dedication to Godwin in the 1818 edition, plus a good deal of literary rumour and speculation, led many of the reviewers to wonder whether or not the author of the novel was in fact P. B. Shelley. The reviewers in *The British Critic* and *The Literary Panorama* betray signs of knowing that the author was Godwin's daughter, but many reviewers and readers assumed a masculine author, some that the author was P. B. Shelley himself.

Walter Scott certainly believed *Frankenstein* to be a product of P. B. Shelley. Scott quotes the lines from P. B. Shelley's 'Mutability' sonnet which are themselves quoted by Frankenstein (volume 2, Chapter 11), just prior to the sublime meeting between creator and creature on the Mer de Glace facing Montanvert and, beyond it, Mont Blanc. The great novelist writes: 'The following lines, which occur in the second volume, mark, we think, that the author pos-sesses the same facility in expressing himself in verse as in prose' (B, p. 305). Scott's important review, however, at once confirms the common features we have been noticing in the contemporary reviews, at the same time that he raises the debate above the level of political and ethical reaction to a consideration of the generic implications of the novel.

Scott's assessment of the generic features and implications of *Frankenstein* centre in his own understanding of the novel's rela-tionship to its Godwinian model. He begins by distinguishing between what we might call 'realist' as opposed to 'romance' or Gothic forms of fiction, before reminding his readers that the latter category of novels, which do not 'bound the events they narrate by the actual laws of nature', divide into at least two distinct approaches. In fact he states that 'the class of marvellous romances admits of several subdivisions'. The main division, however, separates those romances in which 'the marvellous is itself the principal and most important object both to the author and reader' and a 'more philosophical and refined' kind of romance novel, in which 'the laws of nature are represented as altered, not for the purpose of pampering the imagination with wonders, but in order to shew the probable effect which the supposed miracles would produce on those who witnessed them' (B, pp. 300–1). Such novels, Scott argues, attempt to 'open new trains and channels of thought, by placing men in supposed situations of an extraordinary and preternatural character, and then describing the mode of feeling and conduct which they are most likely to adopt' (B, pp. 301–2). Godwin is not yet describing and defining the Godwinian novel, since he asserts, with references to Swift's *Gulliver's Travels*, that the ultimate motivations of such romances can vary. He clarifies the point in the following way:

> We have only to add, that this class of fiction has been sometimes applied to the purposes of political satire, and sometimes to the general illustration of the powers and workings of the human mind. Swift, Bergerac, and others, have employed it for the former purpose, and a good illustration of the latter is the well known Saint Leon of William Godwin. (B, p. 303)

This is an interesting categorization of the Godwinian novel, since it seems to view it as fundamentally philosophical and psychological, rather than political. The account does, however, display a deep understanding of Godwin's 'mental anatomy' approach to fiction making, and it allows him to position *Frankenstein* within that category of novel while avoiding the kinds of political and ideological implications we have seen dictating the thrust of other reviews. Scott continues:

> In this latter work [*St Leon*], assuming the possibility of the transmutation of metals and of the *elixir vitae*, the author had deduced, in the course of his narrative, the probable consequences of the possession of such secrets upon the fortunes

and mind of him who might enjoy them. Frankenstein is a novel upon the same plan with Saint Leon; it is said to be written by Mr Percy Bysshe Shelley, who, if we are rightly informed, is son-in-law to Mr Godwin; and it is inscribed to that ingenious author. (B, p. 303)

Scott's definition of *Frankenstein*, and the Godwinian novel behind it, as an essentially philosophical and psychological form, a kind of novel concerned with opening up our minds to new possibilities for human experience at the same time that it confirms our knowledge about human nature and human behaviour, is one which appears sanctioned by the 1818 anonymous preface. That is to say, Scott may well have felt he was mirroring the author's own expressed aesthetic in his own prefatory description and positioning of *Frankenstein*. He could not have known at the time of writing that things were far more complicated than that.

P. B. SHELLEY'S CRITICAL RESPONSES TO *FRANKENSTEIN*

P. B. Shelley wrote two texts on *Frankenstein*: the 1818 preface and a review which was not published until 1832 in the *Athenæum* (10 November). These texts are in significant ways very different performances, and appear to register rather different responses to the novel. In the sense that P. B. Shelley's preface to the 1818 edition is a response to as well as a description of *Frankenstein*, the novel can be said to include its own critical reception within its pages. We will look at this phenomenon more closely later in this chapter when we consider P. B. Shelley's role in the composition and publication of the novel. As we have seen, a number of the contemporary responses to *Frankenstein* appear to have been directly affected by P. B. Shelley's preface. The anxieties concerning the novel's tendency towards materialism appear in part a response to his account in the first paragraph of the possible if not probable scientific basis of the idea of the human creation of life. He begins: 'The event on which this fiction is founded has been supposed, by Dr. Darwin, and some of the physiological writers of Germany, as not of impossible occurrence' (*1818*, p. vii; see B, p. 47). His comments, as Marilyn Butler has noted, would have been registered by some in the context of the contemporary debate between the dominant (religiously sanctioned) vitalist theories of life and the emergent science of biology, with its materialist account of life (see Butler, *Frankenstein*, pp. ix–li). As Morton notes, citing the debate between John Abernethy and William Lawrence, which Butler has suggested provides a background for *Frankenstein*'s science: 'The debate . . . is pitched around the notion of "organisation." Does life result entirely from its material structure, or is some property or force external to it responsible in some measure?' (Morton, *Frankenstein Sourcebook*, p. 18). The latter view corresponds to the vitalist perspective and, obviously, allows for the presence in nature of a kind of life force attributable to divine origin. The materialist, more secular science of men such as William Lawrence, clearly provoked anxiety within religiously dominated societies such as Britain, so it is not insignificant that P. B. Shelley opens up its possible presence within the novel he is beginning to describe.

P. B. Shelley's preface is not, however, a simple declaration of the novel's scientific as opposed to Christian tendencies. It produces, once we know its authorship, some rather compelling ironies and transformations. P. B. Shelley's ventriloquism of Mary Shelley's authorial voice leads him into areas of the novel which appear to produce a discernible anxiety and hesitancy in his own writing. In the third paragraph, for example, P. B. Shelley writes:

> The opinions which naturally spring from the character and situation of the hero are by no means to be conceived as existing always in my own conviction; nor is any inference justly to be drawn from the following pages as prejudicing any philosophical doctrine of whatever kind. (*1818*, p. x; see B, p. 48)

The last clause is in many respects an extraordinary statement and appears to strip *Frankenstein* of any contribution to thought, to transform it into a mere exercise, along Scott's lines, of the wondrous and the marvellous. *Frankenstein* is a deeply political and philosophical novel, as P. B. Shelley well knew. Why then did he feel the need, before the process of adapting the novel to conventional mores had a chance to begin, to neutralize it in such a fashion?

One answer may be that P. B. Shelley was disturbed by the radicality of the novel his young wife had produced, and was attempting to protect her and her creation from a vituperative critical sphere from which he had frequently suffered. Another answer may come from modern readings of a feminist perspective, such as those influenced by Anne K. Mellor's work, which see in *Frankenstein* a telling critique of the kind of male Romanticism practised by P. B. Shelley himself. A third possibility exists, however. It may be that P. B. Shelley had not as yet had time to assimilate fully the novel that he was prefacing and, rather unused to such an intellectual position of uncertainty, hedged his bets. In 1831, Mary Shelley dated this preface as 'Marlow, September, 1817' and stated that 'As far as I can recollect, it was entirely written by him' (B, p. 358; see also *Frankenstein Notebooks*, vol. 1, p. lxxxviii). A more considered, far less anxious response to *Frankenstein* comes in P. B. Shelley's review, finally published in 1832.

Robinson gives reasons for why P. B. Shelley's review of the novel may have been written in February 1818, one month after the novel's publication (see *Frankenstein Notebooks*, p. xciii). The tone of the review is very different from the preface. P. B. Shelley calls *Frankenstein* 'one of the most original and complete productions of the day', before going on to state explicitly the novel's core message: 'In this the direct moral of the book consists; and it is perhaps the most important, and of the most universal application, of any moral that can be enforced by example. Treat a person ill, and he will become wicked' (B, p. 311). Having established this core moral, P. B. Shelley concludes his review by placing *Frankenstein* squarely within the tradition of the Godwinian novel:

> The Being . . . is, no doubt, a tremendous creature. It was impossible that he should not have received among men that treatment which led to the consequences of his being a social nature. He was an abortion and an anomaly; and though his

mind was such as its first impressions framed it, affectionate and full of moral sensibility, yet the circumstances of his existence are so monstrous and uncommon, that, when the consequences of them became developed in action, his original goodness was gradually turned into inextinguishable misanthropy and revenge. The scene between the Being and the blind De Lacey in the cottage, is one of the most profound and extraordinary instances of pathos that we ever recollect . . . The encounter and argument between Frankenstein and the Being on the sea of ice, almost approaches, in effect, to the expostulation of Caleb Williams with Falkland. It reminds us, indeed, somewhat of the style and character of that admirable writer, to whom the author has dedicated his work, and whose productions he seems to have studied. (B, pp. 311–12)

P. B. Shelley's review confirms the status of *Frankenstein* as a Godwinian novel, yet it also recognizes the ethical challenge posed by the creature. What it also does is to reaffirm some of his own previous interpretations of what Mary Shelley had written, interpretations which exist within the very text of the 1818 and later versions of the novel. Some of P. B. Shelley's early difficulties in responding to *Frankenstein* can perhaps be better understood when we remember the fact of his collaborative participation in its creation. Charles E. Robinson's *Frankenstein Notebooks* provides scholars with a huge resource for studying P. B. Shelley's part in the composition of the novel. Robinson's edition provides facsimiles of the two volumes of the draft copy produced between August and September 1816 to April 1817 and a part of the notebooks in which the Shelleys produced the fair copy of the novel, between April and May 1817.

THE COLLABORATIVE COMPOSITION OF *FRANKENSTEIN*

Robinson provides a rough estimate of 4,000 words which can be traced to P. B. Shelley's pen, as he helped his wife improve and develop the draft and then the fair copy versions of the 1818 text (see *Frankenstein Notebooks*, vol. 1, p. lxviii). Aware of the persistence of unfounded arguments that P. B. Shelley actually wrote the novel himself, arguments (or rumours really) which go back to P. B. Shelley's promotion of his wife's novel, Robinson writes:

> If . . . MWS is the creative genius by which this novel was conceived and developed, we can call PBS an able midwife who helped his wife to bring her monster to life. His 'hand' is in evidence in each of the extent *Frankenstein* Notebooks . . . [and he was also involved, of course] in the printing, publishing, and reviewing of the novel. (*Frankenstein Notebooks*, vol.1, p. lxvii)

Robinson's introduction to the *Frankenstein Notebooks* discusses the various scholarly debates which have revolved around P. B. Shelley's part in the composition of the novel, including important contributions by Anne K. Mellor, James Reiger, E. B. Murray and David Ketterer. The debate necessarily foregrounds issues concerning the persistence of a Romantic idea of individual literary creation (the author as original, as genius, as inspired individual artist) and ideas of collaboration which cut against such Romantic notions. The fact of the matter is that the Shelleys collaborated on a number of projects and clearly, in their daily lives of reading and writing, influenced each other in ways we are still only beginning to understand. Zacharay Leader's fine essay on the issue of creative collaboration shows the manner in which the debate over this issue has moved on from establishing whether P. B. Shelley should be considered a co-author to attempts to understand the precise implications of P. B. Shelley's contribution and Mary Shelley's openness to such contributions.

The attempt to understand P. B. Shelley's contributions to *Frankenstein* produces an exciting new phase in that novel's critical reception. Readers of the draft and fair copy notebooks are confronted with many questions which promise to unsettle radically previous interpretations of the novel radically. Victor, discussing with M. Waldman the merits of the outmoded alchemical writings of Cornelius Agrippa and Paracelsus, is informed by his 'friend' and teacher: 'The labours of men of genius, however erroneously directed, scarcely ever fail in ultimately turning to the solid advantage of mankind' (*1818*, vol. 1,

p. 75; see B, p. 77). What happens to the reader's interpretation of these important words of advice when they discover that they were interpolated into the text by P. B. Shelley? The advice itself sounds like William Godwin promoting the idea that the human faculty of reason must necessarily produce social benefit. Is P. B. Shelley injecting the Godwinian idea of Necessity into Mary Shelley's text, and by so doing tempering her implicit critique of such an idea? It is obvious from the wider context of the novel that M. Waldman's advice is a disastrous gift to offer the young, ambitious Victor Frankenstein. The idea that P. B. Shelley's intention is to inject into the novel an idea of Necessity which the novel squarely rejects appears rather implausible. So we have to consider whether P. B. Shelley is in fact emphasizing Mary Shelley's tempered critique of such a total belief in the powers of human reason and Necessity. Such an interpretation of the addition recognizes that it is an act of reading on P. B. Shelley's part. Changing Mary Shelley's text by reshaping it (with her consent, it should be added), P. B. Shelley is, at the same moment, interpretively reading what she has created. We see this interpretive element of P. B. Shelley's additions and revisions throughout the notebooks.

In the draft of what would become volume 3, Chapter 7, the creature, addressing Walton over the dead body of his creator, asks: 'Why do you not hate Felix who drove his friend from his door or the man who would have destroyed the saviour of his child? Nay they are virtuous and immaculate beings – While I the miserable & . . . trampeled on, am the devil to be spurned & kicked & hated!' P. B. Shelley cancels 'the devil', however, and adds what we now have in both 1818 and 1831: 'an abortion' (*Frankenstein Notebooks*, vol. 2, pp. 638–9). The 1818 version became: 'I, the miserable and the abandoned, am an abortion, to be spurned at, and kicked, and trampled on' (1818, vol. 3, p. 188; *Frankenstein Notebooks*, vol. 2, pp. 638–9). The further changes evidenced there I presume were made at the proof stage. The alteration from 'devil' to 'abortion' is a hugely significant and a brilliantly accurate interpretation, not only of the novel that Mary Shelley had created but also of its relationship with the novels and the political and philosophical writings of her father.

We have, in the previous chapters, encountered this figure of the 'abortive man' on a number of occasions. P. B. Shelley's interpretive sense that the word 'abortion' was philosophically and politically appropriate for this moment of the text suggests how deeply he was responding to the intratextual and intertextual dimensions of Mary Shelley's novel. A whole reading of *Frankenstein* can be built upon the uncanny, rationally disturbing notion of an 'abortive man' and that figure's generation in others (for which read 'us') of 'abhorrence'. If we were to construct such a reading we would have to begin with the recognition that it was a reading which was already there, interpolated into the text itself through P. B. Shelley's deft alteration to a word.

DIFFERENT EDITIONS OF *FRANKENSTEIN*

That studying the notebooks and P. B. Shelley's incorporated interpretation of the novel allows for profoundly new readings of *Frankenstein* is something that has only begun to affect its critical reception. A recognition that readers need to register the differences created by the changes in the text by its republication in 1823 and 1831 is of longer standing and has created a far more diverse critical discussion. The 1818 edition, as we have seen, was the product of the collaborative labour of the Shelleys. The 1823 edition, brought out perhaps to try and capitalize on the first theatrical production of the novel, was managed by Godwin and includes over 120 small changes made by him to the text (see Crook, 'Defence', p. 18). The Thomas copy, referred to by many scholars of the novel's history, concerns the annotated copy Shelley left behind her in Italy in 1823, a copy which demonstrates that she did intend from an early period to produce a revised version of the novel. The 1831 edition was published in Bentley's Standard Novels series and included Shelley's famous introduction. This edition used the 1823 version as copy text and so retained the vast majority of Godwin's minor alterations. It also presented significant major and minor changes by Shelley herself and has been read by many modern critics as radically altering the novel. Anne K.

Mellor writes: 'The 1831 *Frankenstein* is as different from the 1818 *Frankenstein* as Wordsworth's 1850 *Prelude* is different from his 1805 version, and in somewhat the same ways' (Mellor, *Mary Shelley*, p. 170). Mellor's statements here imply that Shelley, like Wordsworth, underwent a personal movement towards conservative politics which significantly altered her great masterpiece and produced what are in effect two novels: the politically radical *1818* and the politically conservative *1831*. The comments also make it clear that the critical debate about the two versions of *Frankenstein* do not simply rest on interpretations of the specific changes Shelley made to her novel; they also rest on a reading of Shelley's biography and the question which has coloured the critical reception of her work since her own lifetime: did Shelley reject the political radicalism of her circle after the deaths of P. B. Shelley and Byron in the early 1820s? Those critics who argue that she did move towards forms of political quietism or conservatism invariably favour *1818* over *1831*. Crook, in her discussion of the debate, cites Mellor, along with Marilyn Butler, Jean de Palacio, James Reiger and Mary Poovey, as examples of such a tendency, and she acknowledges that in Shelley scholarship today this promotion of the 1818 version dominates the critical field. The vast majority of scholarly editions of *Frankenstein* currently available present us with the 1818 text, the 1831 version largely being left to more popular and cheaper reprints of the novel. Having noted that fact, it should also be recognized that in the past 20 years the case for a reassessment of the 1831 version has grown apace and has been supported by an increasing number of Shelley scholars, including Betty T. Bennett, Nora Crook, Elizabeth A. Bohls, Charles E. Robinson, James O'Rourke and David Ketterer. For this later group of scholars, as Crook makes clear, the issue is not one of a choice between *1818* and *1831*, but rather of avoiding the trap of presuming, on the basis of a received 'myth' of Shelley's political backsliding, that *1831* must be a 'tamed' version of *1818*. As Crook states: 'There is no extrinsic evidence, only supposition, that Shelley altered *Frankenstein*, voluntarily or under pressure, in order to accommodate it to Tory and "popular" interpretations' (Crook,

'Defence', p. 4). The debate over the 1818 and 1831 versions is, then, an important one, involving assessments of Shelley's entire literary career and place within the history of nineteenth-century political reformism. Students of the novel need to take the debate seriously and to incorporate a reading of at least some of the changes between the 1818 and the 1831 versions into their overall interpretive response to the novel.

The three volume 1818 version has an epigram from Milton's *Paradise Lost* (Book X, 743–5) on its title page: 'Did I request thee, Maker, from my clay / To mould me man? Did I solicit thee / From darkness to promote me? – ' This epigram is missing from *1831*, a fact which has led some commentators to suggest that Shelley is playing down the potential religious controversy of her story. The fact of the matter is, however, that the epigram was removed by Godwin in the 1823 edition and was not restored by Shelley when she came to revise the text. Why did Shelley not restore the Miltonic epigram? Readers might consider Crook's argument that contemporary reviewers had expressed sympathy with the creature while generally finding little cause for sympathy with Victor. Wishing her readers to experience a problematic, ambivalent sympathy for both Victor and the creature, Shelley, Crook suggests, made numerous small changes to restore some form of sympathy for her eponymous protagonist (see Crook, 'Defence', p. 17). Not beginning the novel by foregrounding the creature's Miltonic associations, might have been a conscious attempt on Shelley's part to create a greater balance in her readers' focus and sympathies.

More significant charges of Shelley's taming her novel in *1831* involve the fact that in that later version Elizabeth is no longer directly related to Victor, instead of being his 'cousin' she is in *1831* a 'foundling' brought into the Frankenstein household. This change, for Mellor, indicates that Shelley is domesticating her representation of the relationship between Elizabeth and Victor, taming the radical 'incestuous overtones' of *1818*, with a more conventionally acceptable portrayal of Elizabeth as 'the Victorian "angel in the house"' (Mellor, *Mary Shelley*, pp. 175–6; see also Butler, *Frankenstein*, p. 200). The point seems plausible, until we are reminded by Crook that '[n]o reviewers had hinted at finding incest in *Frankenstein*. First cousins married each other in early nineteenth-century novels without shocking the public, as in *Mansfield Park*' (Crook, 'Defence', p. 5). A more compelling aspect of Mellor's reading of the 1831 version involves a host of minor and some major changes which appear to foreground the idea of destiny over *1818*'s support for the idea of free will. Mellor writes:

> . . . in *1831*, Mary Shelley reshaped her horror story to reflect her pessimistic conviction that the universe is determined by a destiny blind to human needs or efforts . . . In *1818* Victor Frankenstein possessed free will or the capacity for meaningful moral choice – he could have abandoned his quest for the 'principle of life', he could have cared for his creature, he could have protected Elizabeth. In *1831* such choice is denied him. He is the pawn of forces beyond his knowledge or control. Again and again [in *1831*], Mary Shelley reassigns human actions to chance or fate. (Mellor, *Mary Shelley*, p. 171)

Mellor's comments here appear to be backed up by numerous changes made in the 1831 edition. We have already looked at a major example of *1831*'s apparent foregrounding of destiny over free will in the discussion of passage 2 in Chapter 3 above. For readers like Mellor, the frequent inclusion of figurations of Destiny and Providence into the 1831 *Frankenstein* appears to confirm that the later version is more pessimistic on a philosophical level, more conventionally religious on a social and political level. Butler, like Mellor, talks about the way in which Shelley's 1831 changes 'soften and Christianize Frankenstein's character' (Butler, *Frankenstein*, p. 199). Such readings, however, tend to confuse the words spoken by Victor and characters like Walton and Elizabeth with Shelley's own intentions and beliefs. They do not adequately recognize that Shelley was involved throughout her life in an intense debate with her father's ideas concerning free will and what he called Necessity. As Crook demonstrates, by reference to Godwin's novel *Mandeville* and his philosophical *Thoughts on Man*, published in the same year as the 1831

Frankenstein, Godwin continued to explore the contradictions between the principle of Necessity and free will (Crook, 'Defence', pp. 10–8). Necessity suggests that environmental circumstances dictate human actions; the idea of free will, which appears to be essential to human life, suggests the opposite. As we saw in the first chapter of this book, however, Shelley, throughout her life, criticized the idea, so important to Enlightenment philosophies such as those expressed by Godwin, that the exercise of reason must necessarily promote individual and social benefits (see Allen, *Mary Shelley*). Far from a collapse into a religious and moralistic 'taming' of her previously radical novel, the 1831 *Frankenstein* can be read as a reassertion of that critique of idealistic, overly optimistic forms of Enlightenment thought in the name of a more 'realist' support of social and political reform, a vision of human possibility that does not attempt to wish away the ineradicable presence of tragedy within life. If we return to the alterations at the end of the revised second chapter, we can also see that Shelley in *1831* developed in important ways the reading of her novel inscribed into the 1818 text by P. B. Shelley's interpolated changes. Victor talks about the moment in which 'natural history and all its progeny' became in his mind 'a deformed and abortive creation' (B, p. 327). The 1831 alteration emphasizes, as do a number of other changes, the link we located earlier with the Godwinian idea of the 'abortive man'. Frankenstein's abortive reason may lead him to ascribe the causes of his own and his family and friends' tragedy to the workings of providence and destiny, but the novel's call for a greater level of reason than he, or any of the other central male characters, can provide is sustained and at times increased in the 1831 version.

Crook states that '[t]he perception of Shelley as increasingly politically conservative during the 1830s is at odds with her known sympathies in 1830–1 with radicals such as Frances Wright and Robert Dale Owen, her hopes for the Reform Bill and her growing support for the Italian Risorgimento' (Crook, 'Defence', pp. 5–6). That last reference to the hope for Italian liberation from Austrian rule, is strengthened in the 1831 version by Shelley's alteration of Elizabeth's history. In *1831*, Elizabeth's father, who had in *1818* requested M. Frankenstein to take charge of his motherless daughter given his imminent marriage to an 'Italian lady', becomes himself not only Italian but part of the revolutionary forces:

> The father of their charge [Elizabeth] was one of those Italians nursed in the memory of the antique glory of Italy, – one among the *schiavi ognor frementi* [perpetually restless slaves], who exerted himself to obtain the liberty of his country. He became the victim of its weakness. Whether he had died, or still lingered in the dungeons of Austria, was not known. His property was confiscated, his child became an orphan and a beggar. (B, p. 322)

Belying the idea that Shelley stripped the 1831 version of the novel's former historical and politically topical references, Elizabeth's Milanese father in *1831*, perhaps still lingering in an Austrian prison, reminds readers of the continued oppression of Italy by Austria and of Shelley's support for Italian national liberty. Once we recognize that Shelley did not give up on her peculiar brand of reformist politics in the 1830s we no longer need to make any ideological choice between the 1818 and 1831 versions of *Frankenstein*. In place of that choice we can begin, as some critics have, to trace the fascinating revisions, reinforcements and transformations that *1831* makes to *1818*. Just as we found a mode of critical reading incorporated into *1818*, so *1831* can be understood as another stage in that ongoing, internal re-reading of Shelley's story.

PUBLICATION HISTORY OF *FRANKENSTEIN*

Shelley's reading of her own text is a fascinating subject. But what of Shelley's other readers? The 1818 edition of *Frankenstein*, published by Lackington, Hughes, Harding, Mavor and Jones, printed 500 copies at the expensive price of the standard three volume novel. The 1823 edition was a small one in terms of print size. One would imagine, then, that it was with the Bentley edition of 1831 that *Frankenstein* gained a wider, mass audience. The story of Bentley's handling of his Standard Novels series is told in William St Clair's *The Reading Nation in the Romantic Period*. Although Bentley successfully drew a large number of the novels of the Romantic period into his series, the new paratextual material of introductions and revisions allowing him to gain copyright over these novels for decades afterwards, his publishing firm never fully embraced the phenomenon of the cheap popular paperback which revolutionized the publishing world after the 1830s. Comparing the cheap versions of Walter Scott's novels to those in Bentley's series, St Clair writes: 'Whereas, in the case of the Waverley novels, the further lowering of prices took the texts to a reading nation of several millions, in the case of the other novels of the period [in Bentley's control], readership remained confined to the upper tranches' (*Reading Nation*, p. 364). This situation led to *Frankenstein* being out of print, with the odd exception, throughout the 1850s, 1860s and 1870s. Not until the 1880s, when it came out of its previous copyright restrictions, did *Frankenstein* finally reach the reading public it was always destined to find. As St Clair notes: 'In its first year, the first reprint of *Frankenstein* sold more copies than all of the previous editions put together . . . At the turn of the nineteenth century, eighty years after its first appearance, *Frankenstein* at last became accessible to the whole reading nation' (*Reading Nation*, p. 365).

Frankenstein has remained a popular, widely read novel ever since, in the past 30 years or so graduating ever more completely into school classes, university lecture halls and seminar rooms, discussed in numerous academic papers, essays and books. The history of Bentley's copyright possession of the novel, however, reminds us that, as St Clair puts it, '[d]uring most of the nineteenth century it was not the reading of the text of the book, but seeing adaptations of the story on the stage which kept *Frankenstein* alive in culture' (*Reading Nation*, p. 367). That unique history of adaptation, in theatrical, cinematic and other cultural forms is discussed in the next chapter.

In the next chapter, along with an analysis of the history of adaptations of *Frankenstein* and its ongoing influence, we will look at modern critical interpretations of Mary Shelley's novel.

STUDY QUESTIONS

1. Look at the list of substantive variants appended to the Broadview edition of the 1818 *Frankenstein* (pp. 316–52) or another scholarly edition containing the variants and locate at least five significant alterations (these can be on the level of words, whole sentences or paragraphs). Explain how those changes help to address the question of whether the 1831 version is or is not a politically conservative 'taming' of the 1818 version.
2. Read the reviews included in the Broadview edition (pp. 300–12) and P. B. Shelley's 1818 'Preface' (pp. 47–8) and explain how they agree and disagree about the novel's meaning and motivation.

CHAPTER 5

ADAPTATION, INTERPRETATION AND INFLUENCE

THEATRICAL ADAPTATIONS OF *FRANKENSTEIN*

On 22 July 1823 Godwin wrote to his daughter about plans for a theatrical production of *Frankenstein* in London:

> It is a curious circumstance that a play is just announced, to be performed at the English Opera House in the Strand next Monday, entitled Presumption, or the Fate of Frankenstein. I know not whether it will succeed. If it does, it will be some sort of feather in the cap of the author of the novel, a recommendation in your future negociaions [sic] with booksellers. (see Forry, p. 3)

Shelley at this time was preparing to return to England, a widow with one remaining child. By 18 August, Shelley had reached Paris, and was able to inform Leigh Hunt that the theatrical adaptation of her novel was not so frightening to 'the ladies' as had been expected and that the piece was 'having a run' (Mary Shelley, *Letters*, vol. 1, p. 374). In another letter to Hunt, dated in the second week of September, Shelley describes her reaction to attending a performance of Richard Brinsley Peake's *Presumption; or, The Fate of Frankenstein*:

> But lo & behold! I found myself famous! – Frankenstein had prodigious success as a drama & was about to be repeated for the 23rd night at the English opera house . . . The story is not

well managed – but [Thomas Potter] Cooke played —'s part extremely well – his seeking as it were for support – his trying to grasp at the sounds he heard – all indeed he does was well imagined & executed. I was much amused, & it appeared to excite a breathless eagerness in the audience . . . & all stayed till it was over. They continue to play it even now. (Mary Shelley, *Letters*, vol. 1, p. 378)

Peake's *Presumption* was indeed a 'prodigious success'; it was performed 37 times in its first 1823 run and went on to be regularly revived up until the 1840s (Forry, pp. 10–11). *Presumption* is a melodrama, and as such it radically alters Shelley's novel, helping to begin the process of creating that alternative version of *Frankenstein* which developed alongside the novel's reception for the next two centuries. In Peake's play the nameless creature is returned back to his stock position as a non-speaking 'monster', the laboratory assistant Fritz (so important in the later films) is introduced, along with a number of tableaux which will influence many of the later theatrical adaptations and eventually the twentieth-century film versions. For example, in Act 1, scene 3, as Fritz peeps into Frankenstein's blue-lit laboratory through a 'small lattice window', his master is heard to exclaim 'It lives! It lives!', a scene which James Whale's 1931 film version will take from offstage and place at the visual centre of the cinematic tradition of *Frankenstein* adaptations (see Forry, p. 143). Peake's foregrounding of the word 'presumption' from the 1818 text helped to establish a tradition of moralizing and Christianizing the story by, in equal parts, silencing the creature's pleas for sympathy and justice, and turning Victor himself into an exercise in the classic, male overreacher. Peake's play inspired a series of melodramatic and burlesque versions of the story, including John Atkinson Kerr's *The Monster and Magician; or, The Fate of Frankenstein* and Henry M. Milner's *The Man and the Monster; or, The Fate of Frankenstein* (1826).

Forry, in his excellent study of the history of stage adaptations of *Frankenstein*, lists 16 different theatrical adaptations from 1821 to 1826, nine of them in the year 1826, and 19 in all up to the end of the 1880s (see also Morton, *Frankenstein Sourcebook*, pp. 59–63). As Forry states: 'In the course of three years, from 1823 to 1826, at least fifteen dramas employed characters and themes from Shelley's novel. Whether in burlesque or melodrama, things Frankensteinian were all the rage on stages in England and France' (Forry, p. 34). Forry's work also confirms the arguments put forward by Baldick and others about the mutating significance of *Frankenstein* in popular and political culture. By the 1830s, as British society entered the age of the Reform Bill and a series of social crises, the adaptation of *Frankenstein* took on new, frequently political and politicized forms. As Forry argues, the influence of the 'Frankenstein myth' seems, in the 1830s through to the 1880s, to have moved from the popular theatre into the controversial realm of the political cartoon. Baldick, Forry and Morton include within their studies a number of contemporary political cartoons, all of which exploit the tale of Frankenstein to speak to and often to exploit popular anxieties and fears, or to visually satirize the actions of political figures and groups. The cartoon entitled 'Frankenstein's Creating Peers' from *McLean's Monthly Sheet of Characters* (1 March 1832), for example, satirizes William IV's consent in creating a rack of new peers who would be willing to pass the Reform Bill (see Forry, p. 44). Later cartoons, dealing with a restless working class, the possible consequences of the Crimean War, the unrest in Ireland during the famine-ridden 1840s or the emergence of Irish Fenianism in the later part of the century, demonstrate the story's potentiality for articulating the fears of conservative society regarding a series of potentially violent groups 'outside' of legitimate society. *Frankenstein*'s ability to speak to dominant society's anxiety over the unification of previously disorganised and muted sections of society is powerfully conveyed in such political images (see Forry, pp. 43–53).

CINEMATIC ADAPTATIONS OF *FRANKENSTEIN*

Both forms of nineteenth-century adaptation discussed so far share a transformation of Shelley's original text into visual forms. T. P. Cooke and another actor, O. Smith, hugely enhanced their reputations (along with their notoriety) by performing the part of the creature in the most important 1820s theatrical versions. In the twentieth century, of course, this visualization of Shelley's novel continued, but now in the context of a century in which the visual image came to dominate human society as never before. Glut and Florescu provide excellent guides to the numerous *Frankenstein* films produced in the twentieth century, and from their work, along with other studies, it is possible to discern within the daunting, international variety of cinematic adaptations a number of cycles in this tradition. There seems to be something about Shelley's novel which makes film-makers and audiences return to it again and again. Early pioneers of the moving image, for example, seem to have recognized that the emerging art of cinema possessed a literary correlative in Victor's animation of his creature. Glut discusses the Thomas A. Edison film company's 1910 silent *Frankenstein*, with its disturbing representation of the creature played by Charles Ogle (Glut, pp. 58–63). He then goes on to discuss the Ocean Film Corporation's 1915 *Life without Soul* before examining the manner in which German-based cinema, in the 1910s and 1920s, produced a series of related Golem films (in which an artificial man is animated into life), the most important of which remains the 1920s *Der Golem: Wie er in die Welt Kam* ('The Golem: How He Came Into The World'), directed and starring Paul Wegener (Glut, pp. 63–7, 67–85). The most abiding testament to the manner in which the idea of Frankensteinian animation spoke to the earliest film-makers and audiences, however, probably lies in a film which does not directly cite Shelley's novel, Fritz Lang's *Metropolis* (1926) with its mad scientist Rotwang creating a subversive female robot, Maria, in a compellingly visualized futuristic world. *Metropolis* requires mention here because its influence can be registered throughout the rest of the century and into the twenty-first century. This influence concerns film's ability to combine the representation of artificial life with hypothetical, but sometimes brilliantly realized, future worlds in which the borders between humanity and technology are radically shifted and even broken down. We will return to that cinematic tradition at the end of this chapter when we discuss the broader social and cultural influence of *Frankenstein*.

The second discernible wave of *Frankenstein* films centres on the work produced by the US company Universal Pictures, in the 1930s and the 1940s. The story of how James Whale, the young British director in Hollywood, came to film Boris Karloff's iconic version of Shelley's creature has become part of film history. Karloff's heavy, angular make-up, created by Jack Pierce, has itself become a cultural myth which it is quite impossible to avoid or forget. Colin Clive's hysterical rendition of [Henry] Frankenstein's act of creation, transforming Peake's version into a maniacal 'It's alive! It's alive!', is also an enduring moment of cinematic history, produced as it is in a laboratory in which science now appears to be spiralling out of control. A very rewarding discussion of the manner in which the Universal films developed the nineteenth-century theatrical adaptations of Shelley's novel is provided in Albert J. Lavalley's 'The Stage and Film Children of *Frankenstein*'.

The 1931 Universal film inaugurated what we might call the modern *Frankenstein* industry. Universal studios in the next two decades produced a series of *Frankenstein* films, beginning with the superior *Bride of Frankenstein* (1935) (also starring Karloff and directed by Whale), on to *Son of Frankenstein* (1939) and a number of other 1940s remakes in which various horror figures (such as the Wolfman, Dracula, and the Mummy) are brought into sometimes humorous, frequently parodic collisions, and the bankable talents of comedy duo Abbot and Costello are also let loose on material less to do with horror and more to do with spoof and slapstick. If we understand Whale's two Universal *Frankenstein* films as adaptations of Shelley's novel, then the obvious question becomes what new, contemporary meaning is generated by these films' re-reading or re-visioning of the original novel (and of course the theatrical tradition which mediates in between)? To what socio-political contexts do Whale's two films adapt the story of *Frankenstein*? Esther Schor states that these 'films both reflect and refract their own historical moment . . . In the history of Frankenstein films, we can trace a Rorschach – a psychologist's inkblot – of our collective fears' (Schor, p. 64). She goes on to argue that Whale's films concern racism and lynching (in the case of *Frankenstein*), and eugenics and the threat of nuclear war (in the case of *Bride*). In an influential essay entitled 'Production and Reproduction: The Case of *Frankenstein*', Paul O'Flinn argues that Whale's 1931 film is a deeply reactionary response to the social turmoil created by the Great Depression of the 1930s. In his reading, the radical sympathy created in Shelley's novel for the creature is greatly reduced (Whale's creature, after all, is given an 'abnormal' brain by mistake), and an anxiety over the possibility of mob violence, hardly traceable in the novel, is accentuated in its adaptation into the mass media of the cinema. O'Flinn writes:

> What Universal's *Frankenstein* seeks to say specifically to the mass audience at whom it is aimed concerns above all mass activity in times of crisis: where that activity might be assertive and democratic and beneficial (the Walton story), it is removed and concealed; where it is violent and insurrectionary (the monster's story), it is systematically denigrated; and where it is traditional and reactionary (the mill-burning), it is ambiguously endorsed. The extent to which the film powerfully articulates those familiar stances of the dominant ideology in the 1930s is measured by its box-office success. (O'Flinn, p. 39)

Whale's 1931 *Frankenstein* is still one of the most financially successful films ever made, costing a mere $250,000 to produce and grossing over $12,000,000. While O'Flinn's reading of Whale's 1931 film appears reasonable, it also seems to leave a good deal out of the picture. Although interpretations of such films in terms of social anxieties are obvious enough, it is worth remembering that a great proportion of the audience for such films would have found pleasure in the idea of scientific innovation (see James, p. 91). We return here to Shelley's novel and its ability to generate contrasting political and ideological readings. Whale's two *Frankenstein* films have a similar capacity. Against O'Flinn's reading of the 1931 film, for example, David Punter argues that 'much of the complexity of Mary Shelley's text remains present in the film' (Punter, *Literature of Terror*, vol. 2, p. 99). Far from reducing the audience's sympathy for the creature, as O'Flinn suggests Whale's 1931 film does, Glut and others argue that Karloff's visual rendering of the creature only goes to heighten that sympathetic response. If one remembers other political and economic issues dominant in the USA in the 1930s, such as the foreign policy of isolationism, it is possible to generate further readings of Whale's films in which they present a warning against or a promotion of such a national policy.

Some of the most compelling readings of Whale's *Frankenstein* and *Bride* take us back to the manner in which Shelley's novel allows cinema to reflect upon and examine its own nature as a new medium of representation. We might start here with Schor's statement: 'The heart of the matter is what movies do that the novel cannot do: show us the monster' (Schor, p. 65). William Nestrick, for example, discusses the manner in which early film-makers frequently associated themselves with magicians and with those mythic figures capable of animation, of summoning ghosts or of bringing things back to life. We can say of cinema what Roland Barthes so movingly suggested of photography in his *Camera Lucida*, that they are media in which the dead can return. In discussing these early responses to the moving image, therefore, Nestrick provides us with a major clue as to the apparently unending fascination the film industry displays for Shelley's novelistic masterpiece. As he states: 'The special way in which the medium of film engages [the] myth of animation can be seen in its persistent return to the literary source of *Frankenstein*' (Nestrick, pp. 291–2). Nestrick's approach allows us to see a deeper connection than the adaptation to contemporary political issues between Shelley's novel and Whale's Universal films. Frankenstein's re-animation of the dead becomes, in such an approach, a metaphor by and through which film can reflect on its own apparently magical capacity to recreate life, to make static images move, to bring back into the collective present past moments, past words, past lives. The additions Whale made to *Bride*, in particular Dr Praetorius playing 'gods and monsters' with his tiny, mainly aristocratic and bourgeois miniature people, suddenly begin to appear newly illuminated by such a reading. When audiences flocked to see *Frankenstein* and *Bride* they were not simply pleasurably horrified by the idea of a scientific triumph over nature;

they also no doubt were thrilled by the new, technological media of film itself. Michael Grant writes of the 1931 film: 'The film concerns itself with the process of creation and the consequences of it, a process that involves not only Frankenstein's creation of the monster but also the articulation whereby the film itself comes into being' (Grant, p. 116).

Recognizing that *Frankenstein* functions as a mirror for cinema's own representational capacities and technological triumph over time (its ability to bring back the dead, to re-animate) should not lead us away from the socio-political and ideological nature of *Frankenstein* films, however. This point is confirmed if we look at what we might call the third cycle in the cinematic adaptation of Shelley's novel. By the end of the 1940s Universal Pictures had wrung as much life as it could out of Frankenstein and his creature. In the period between the 1950s and the 1970s Shelley's novel came home, as it were, in a new series of Frankenstein films produced by the London-based studio, Hammer Films. *The Curse of Frankenstein*, directed by Terence Fisher and starring Peter Cushing as Frankenstein and Christopher Lee as the creature, was released by Hammer in 1957. The film, as Peter Hutchings puts it, 'inaugurated the British horror boom and established Fisher as a film-maker whose name was known to critics, if only as someone who specialised in the despised horror genre' (Hutchings, p. 81). Over the next two decades, Hammer went on to produce numerous horror movies, including six subsequent *Frankenstein* films. Five of these *Frankenstein* adaptations (*Curse, Revenge, Frankenstein Created Woman, Frankenstein Must Be Destroyed, Frankenstein and the Monster from Hell*) were directed by Fisher, who had already directed a film on the subject of reanimation in his 1953 *Four Sided Triangle*. Fisher's Hammer films can legitimately be described as a new phase in the cinematic tradition of adapting Shelley's novel, since they form a coherent series which place the focus on Frankenstein himself (in all of Fisher's films played by Peter Cushing) and generally relegate the creature to the status of a theme, in particular the transplantation of human identities (whether that be understood in terms of soul, brain, mind, genius and talent, or even gender). It is, then, somewhat easier to make claims about the social significance of Fisher's *Frankenstein* films. Notorious and often critically censured for their gore, Fisher's films seem to plug into various contemporary issues: the medical advances in heart and other organ transplants associated with the work of Christian Barnard; the rise in the social and cultural importance of the figure of the doctor within the context of the new National Health Service in Britain; and, perhaps most significantly, after the horrors of World War Two, the possibility of a man who is both truly amoral and yet also truly enlightened, in the sense of his scientific and even humanistic education and knowledge. Peter Cushing, as all commentators have noted, towers over everything else in Fisher's Hammer *Frankenstein* films. He has been described as a return to the amoral, Byronic figure of which Shelley had intimate knowledge in her own time (see David Pirie); but he can seem more like the expression of a wholly twentieth-century response to the collapse of what Jurgen Habermas calls 'the project of Modernity'.

If Modernity, or the Enlightenment, dominant in philosophical and political thought since the eighteenth century, would have us believe that reason and social progress are inextricably linked (that the more we as individuals and as a society learn the more we will liberate ourselves), how are we to continue to believe in the necessity of such a link after the unimaginable inhumanity and genocide of World War Two and the rise of Nazism within apparently enlightened Europe? This question is perhaps the most profound one facing philosophy, politics and science in the latter part of the twentieth and now in the twenty-first century. It might seem a rather improbable context within which to introduce Fisher's popularistic, gore-ridden shockers, so saturated as they are in the discourses of mainstream cinema and television. It does not seem a long jump, after all, from Fisher's series to the often hilarious 1966 *Carry On Screaming*, and indeed that association might foreground a persistent feature of these films. Just as the *Carry On* team of the 1960s and 1970s (some of whom also appeared in Hammer horror films) revelled in adopting 'foreign' settings and clothing (the source of laughter to their almost exclusively British audience), so Fisher's films constantly play and pun on the language and names (place and person) of their European, mainly Germanic, settings. David Punter, following David Pirie, talks about 'the "British-ness" of the sources with which the Hammer films deal' (Punter, vol. 2, p. 108). It remains notable, however, that much of the films' irony was generated by the cultural hybridity created by their European locations and 'sources'. A linguistic play on Germanic names such as Hans, Kleve, Carlsbad (Karlsbad), Hertz, and so forth runs throughout Fisher's films and appears to produce a covert level of meaning under the more surface, moralistic level of evil scientists manipulating innocent victims. In *Frankenstein Created Woman*, for example, the doctor's hands, burnt by the fire of previous films and damaged by overuse, are useless for the purpose of his secret, scientific work. He therefore employs assistants. Frankenstein relies on his good-natured but uncomprehending assistant Dr Hertz to do this surgery. He requires Dr Hertz (*herz* is the German word for heart) to be his hands. Dr Hertz explains to the physically restored Christine Kleve, 'The hands were mine, but the skill was his.' Hans (love interest for Christine), was also one of Frankenstein's 'hands' (nineteenth-century term for a factory worker) until his execution by the guillotine. Frankenstein, with the help of Dr Hertz's hands, eventually places Hans's mind within Christine's reanimated body (she had committed suicide after Hans's decapitation). Throughout the rest of the film, literally carrying Hans's head inside her own, Christine takes orders from the voice of Hans; she becomes his 'hands' in the kind of revenge story which John McCarty says is typical of the plot of many Hammer films. The film culminates in Christine Kleve, Hans-in-head, taking revenge on the upper-class, dissolute murderers of her lover, Hans (for further evidence of the Fisher films' play on 'hands', see Darryl Jones, p. 55). A play on the word 'Kleve' (in English 'cleaver' but also 'to cleave' *qua* be faithful) develops in this and other Fisher *Frankenstein* films. This brief synopsis of *Frankenstein Created Woman* demonstrates something of the force of the British/ European hybridity of Fisher's Frankenstein films. It also allows us to glimpse the manner in which the British class system is fed into and through the play between British and

European (Germanic) linguistic and narrative features, encouraging British audiences to identify with the often Cockney-sounding working-class publicans, asylum workers, landladies or more neutrally 'English' sounding protagonists like Hans, and marking the distance between the audience and upper-class (and thus 'foreign') villains including, ultimately, Peter Cushing's authoritative and often authoritarian accented Frankenstein.

Cushing's Frankenstein is, however, an ambivalent character. Superior to everyone around him in terms of education and intellect, he is nonetheless ousted and frequently hunted by respectable upper-class society. A recurrent theme of waste (of human spirit, talent, knowledge and genius) can perhaps help us understand this ambivalence of character a little more. In *Curse*, the dream of Frankenstein is to create a creature with 'a lifetime of knowledge behind it'. This is why he chooses to murder Professor Bernstein, 'the greatest brain in Europe'. In *Frankenstein Must Be Destroyed*, as he tries to explain the ultimate goal of his and Dr Brandt's research, Frankenstein expresses the philosophical, Enlightenment dimension of his research. In the film, he says:

> We were seeking to preserve for all time the great talents and geniuses of the world. When they die their brains are at the height of their creative power. And we bury them under the ground to rot because the bodies that house them have worn out. We want to remove those brains at the instant of death and freeze them, thus preserving for posterity all they contain.

Karl, his assistant, responds: 'It's frightening!' But why so? Frankenstein's words here, after all, could be said to summarize the basic tenets of the project of Modernity since the eighteenth century. Is Frankenstein's vision here related to the fascist dream of purity which led to the death camps and the final solution? Or is this the project of Enlightenment which was and still is supposed to protect us from that kind of historical nightmare? Is Frankenstein a Nazi doctor, or is he an Enlightenment intellectual who wants to preserve the greatest achievement of European civilization?

In *Frankenstein and the Monster From Hell,* Dr Victor (Frankenstein's name changes through the films since he has to continue to escape from the consequences of his past actions) is at once a mad, Nazi-like doctor (splicing the hands of a craftsman with the head of a genius and the preternaturally strong body of a 'throwback' Neanderthal man) *and* he is a GP, carefully nurturing his patients, taking all the time in the world over their physical needs. The entire film takes place in the State Asylum for the Criminally Insane. In this film Frankenstein has found a world, an entire social space in which to conduct his research. Frankenstein is master here, knowing the terrible secret of the clearly alcoholic Director's addiction to pornography, knowing the terrible secret of the Director's attempted rape of his own daughter, the mute Sarah (Madeline Smith), whom everyone calls 'The Angel'. Knowing all this, and yielding the power of his superior intellect, Frankenstein in this setting is a dictator. But he is also the source of order, of humanity and of care.

Frankenstein's assistant this time is the young Simon Helder, who has been sentenced to the asylum for conducting experiments which seek to emulate those of Frankenstein. The Judge says, on sentencing him: 'If we cannot trust even our so called enlightened men of science to behave in a manner proper to a decent and God-fearing citizen then who can we trust?' Dr Helder thinks he knows the answer, trusting in Frankenstein as a scientist rather than a God-fearing man; and he continues in this trust until Frankenstein suggests that they take the creature (Professor Durendel's brain, and Herr Talmut's hands, in Herr Schnider's monstrous, Neanderthal body) and mate him with 'The Angel'. This is a shocking idea even to Dr Helder: 'You cannot', he says, 'divorce science and humanity to that extent'. Frankenstein, to the foreground, simply closes his eyes; he has heard it all before. Besides, what is he supposed to do about such a divorce, such a cleavage? He is, as he always was, dedicated to his work; that is what he knows and what he is. He is a kind of machine, as the end of this film makes perfectly clear: he is a machine, a workaholic, who wants to create life, to improve life, to eradicate the waste of 'life'. He wants to bring the best minds and the best hands and the best bodies together: he is a scientist, a man of Enlightenment. He is also – and perhaps beyond anything else this is where his fascination and ambivalence lies – single-minded.

Paul Leggett has argued that in *Curse* 'Frankenstein's whole perspective is devoid of moral scruple' (Leggett, p. 17). In fact, as we have seen, Cushing's Frankenstein, in his single-minded, pure and yet murderous pursuit of knowledge and the eradication of human waste, mirrors back to us fundamental concerns about human endeavour which are in many ways far more directly related to the ethics of Shelley's original novel than anything produced by and in Whale's more globally acknowledged Universal adaptations. Are human beings ever capable of being single-minded? Or does the honourable desire to improve human knowledge and technological abilities always go hand-in-hand with the 'animalistic' qualities of ruthlessness and unconcern for the individual? This moral ambiguity can also be read as a self-conscious exploration of the very kind of horror film which made the career of Fisher. Far more philosophical than Universal's *Frankenstein* films, Fisher's films also evince a troubling pleasure in decapitation, dismemberment and explicit violence. They are films which appear to utilize the ambivalence of Frankenstein's own character to explore their own moral ambivalence as horror films, at once philosophical and yet bordering on the pornographic. Once again, in Fisher's hands, *Frankenstein* proves itself to be a text which allows horror cinema to reflect upon its own abilities to provoke the intellect at the same time as speaking to base emotions.

Discussing *Frankenstein* on film in terms of a series of cycles does not, of course, allow for the numerous one-off adaptations that have continued to keep Shelley's novel on the large and the smaller screen. Often discussed films include the Andy Warhol's erotic *Flesh For Frankenstein* (1973), the camp musical *The Rocky Horror Picture Show* (1975), Mel Brooks's hilarious horror film spoof *Young Frankenstein* (1974), Ken Russell's excessive rendition of the events in the Via Diodati, *Gothic*

(1986), *Frankenstein Unbound* (1990), Roger Corman's film adaptation of Brian Aldiss's novel of the same name and Kenneth Branagh's much anticipated but somewhat disappointing *Mary Shelley's 'Frankenstein'* (1994). None of these films, save for Mel Brook's comic masterpiece, are as interesting as those produced by Universal and Hammer, and pale beside more loosely, but often just as significantly, related sci-fi films which I will discuss at the end of this chapter.

MODERN CRITICAL INTERPRETATIONS OF *FRANKENSTEIN*

In following the history of film adaptations of *Frankenstein* we learn much about the nature of film itself. Likewise, coming to terms with the vast array of critical interpretations of Shelley's novel over the past 35 years or so tells us a great deal about the nature of modern literary and cultural criticism. It would be possible, for example, to chart most of the transformations within feminist criticism over that period by looking at the numerous readings of Shelley's novel produced by feminist critics. Mary Poovey, Gilbert and Gubar, Anne K. Mellor and others have explored Shelley's relation to the male-dominated tradition of literary writing in ways which exemplify the leading concerns and characteristics of British and US feminist criticism in the 1970s and 1980s. More recently, younger feminist critics, like Mitzi Myers, reflecting new ideas about the position of women writers within the public sphere, have questioned 'the pervasive binarism' which assumes a purely antagonist relationship between a male public and a female private sphere. This questioning of what Myers calls 'spherist' arguments can be seen to be part of a recent move in feminist criticism to register the aesthetic and ideological authority of writers such as Mary Shelley, rather than concentrating on their struggle with and against an apparently monolithic masculine culture and masculine forms (see Bennett, 'Feminism and Editing', pp. 67–89).

Just as *Frankenstein* criticism reflects changes in feminist thought and work, any attempt to gain an overview of interpretations of Shelley's novel over this period has to come to terms with the major changes within literary theory and criticism generally (for a discussion see Hoeveler). We can see this more clearly if we attend to some of the most important essay collections dedicated to *Frankenstein*. Some of these collections clearly struggle with the sheer diversity of interpretations that *Frankenstein* has produced. An example can be found in Harold Bloom's *Mary Shelley* (1985), a collection dominated by essays on *Frankenstein* which does not seem to be able to find any coherent way of linking together its assembly of traditional accounts (Spark, Nelson, Jr, Walling) with approaches leading off in the different directions of genre theory (Levine), psychoanalytical theory (Brooks and Sherwin), and the feminist reading of Gilbert and Gubar. In his more recent collection on *Frankenstein*, Bloom takes a different, just as problematic tack. A series of brief passages from critical works ranging from Scott's review to Hill-Miller's 1995 book on Shelley and Godwin, all serve to justify Bloom's rather contestable reading of *Frankenstein*'s 'central paradox': 'which is that the "daemon", or creature, is no monster, but that his creator, Dr Victor Frankenstein, pragmatically is a moral idiot' (Bloom, *Mary Shelley's 'Frankenstein'*, p. 4).

Other collections organize themselves in differing ways in attempts to guide their readers through the various interpretative roads down which *Frankenstein* has taken its readers. The still hugely important, seminal collection, *The Endurance of 'Frankenstein'*, edited by George Levine and U. C. Knoepflmacher, arranges its essays into five sections: essays which revise traditional readings of the novel (Levine, Wilt, Griffin); biographical readings of a feminist and gender orientation (Moers, Knoepflmacher); cultural and political readings (Ellis, Sterrenburg, Scott); approaches which focus on language, psychoanalysis and genre (Brooks, Stevick); and essays dealing with the stage and film adaptations of *Frankenstein* (Lavalley, Nestrick). It is interesting to note, in such an important contribution to the re-evaluation of *Frankenstein* and Shelley generally, that the editors appear uncertain about the aesthetic quality of the novel they are celebrating. Levine, for example, states at the beginning of his essay: 'Of course, *Frankenstein* is a "minor" novel, radically flawed by its sensationalism, by the inflexibly public and oratorical nature of even its most intimate passages.

But it is, arguably, the most important minor novel in English' (Levine, 'Ambiguous Heritage', p. 3). Within a decade it would become practically impossible for serious scholars of the novel to make such a statement about *Frankenstein*'s aesthetic value. In their collection, Levine and Knoepflmacher were in fact helping to establish a reassessment of *Frankenstein* which would quickly come to position it as one of the most important literary works of the Romantic period.

Collections of the 1990s demonstrate how radically *Frankenstein* criticism grew and diversified through the 1980s and beyond. Johanna M. Smith's Bedford Books edition of the 1831 *Frankenstein* is designed to help students negotiate their way through the complexities of modern literary theory and criticism. The collection of essays it contains draws an explicit relation between modern interpretations of *Frankenstein* and the diverse state of modern literary and cultural theory and practice. Smith divides this collection into five categories, each one with a general reading list and a more specific list of critical applications on *Frankenstein*, before providing one complete essay as example. Her categories are reader-response theory (Lowe-Evans), psychoanalysis (Collings), feminism (Smith herself), Marxism (Montag) and cultural criticism (Heller). Smith's approach is useful in that it provides very detailed introductions and guides to students coming to these theoretical approaches for the first time. Her collection, however, does not cover the full extent of theoretical approaches which have been applied to *Frankenstein*. Fred Botting's New Casebook collection, published only three years after Smith's edition, extends the range of interpretative approaches considerably, presenting a selection of readings which begin to give readers an accurate impression of the diversity of reading practices now being applied to Shelley's novel: psychoanalysis (Brooks); feminism (Mellor, Homans); Marxism (O'Flinn); cultural criticism (Baldick); structural analysis (Kestner); deconstructive criticism (Newman, Freeman); post-structuralism (Hogle); post-colonial criticism (Spivak).

The expansion of critical and theoretical focus observable in Smith's and Botting's collections is increased once again when we come to collections published since 2000. Charting *Frankenstein* criticism through the 1970s, 1980s and 1990s provides us with a very clear example of the manner in which theoretical approaches (structuralist, post-structuralist, feminist, psychoanalytical, deconstructive, post-Marxist, post-colonial, new historical) gained ever greater importance in those decades. Collections since 2000 demonstrate, however, that, in the UK and the USA at least, a certain consolidation around historical, cultural and political approaches has also occurred. Both Schoene-Harwood's and Morton's recent *Frankenstein* collections are dominated by a critical agenda which we might label under the rather loose umbrella term 'new historicist'. Beginning with a chapter on the traditional reception of *Frankenstein*, Schoene-Harwood goes on to present an interesting and extremely useful book in which extracts from some of the most important modern interpretations are explained and related. Schoene-Harwood's interpretive collection maps modern *Frankenstein* criticism through various thematic chapters: Shelley's struggle with her intellectual and political heritage in essays by Elizabeth Bronfen, and James Carlson, and James O'Rourke's essay on Shelley and Rousseau; the manner in which Devon Hodges, among others, uses psychoanalytical approaches to understand the often antagonistic relationship between literary and critical texts; essays on the representation of gender by Burton Hatlen and Colleen Hobbs among others; readings of the political, ideological and medical significances of the figure of monstrosity, including those by Paulson, Bewell and Alan Rauch; and finally, readings of the scientific and cinematic heritage of the novel by critics such as Raymond Hammond, Thomas Frentz and Janice Rushing.

Morton's collection of essays perhaps demonstrates even more clearly the current predominance of cultural, political and historical approaches. In the section of his book on 'Modern Criticism', Morton divides interpretations of *Frankenstein* into six sections: (i) the body, medicine and science; (ii) commodity culture and social structure; (iii) gender and queer theories; (iv) genre, literary form and literary history; (v) language and psyche; (vi) race, colonialism and orientalism. This is a very rewarding map of the interpretive routes which modern critical readers of Shelley's novel have explored. Morton emphasizes many of the most innovative approaches to the novel, including the analysis, inspired by Marilyn Butler and others, of Shelley's intervention into contemporary scientific debates. This topic, as he states, extends out to 'issues of materiality and the physical universe' (Morton, *Frankenstein Sourcebook*, p. 80) and includes books on Romantic science by Morton himself, along with Tim Marshall's fascinating account of *Frankenstein* and the legacy of grave-robbing and dissection. Morton also includes extracts from important and still influential readings on gender by Mary Jacobus, Eve Kosofsky Sedgwick and Barbara Johnson, and on race by Elizabeth A. Bohls and H. L. Malchow.

THE INFLUENCE OF *FRANKENSTEIN*

What Morton's and Schoene-Harwood's collections also have in common is a recognition that *Frankenstein*'s influence on and utilization by modern science (whether that be fictional or factual or a mixture of the two) is a subject of serious and often quite profound critical, artistic and scientific interpretation and practice. A similar recognition structures Stephen Bann's 1994 collection of essays, *Frankenstein, Creation and Monstrosity*. In his 1998 book on science and genetics, Jon Turney takes *Frankenstein* as the organizational hub of his text because, as he states: 'Mary Shelley's *Frankenstein* has long been a versatile frame for interpreting our relationship with technology . . . Her story about finding the secret of life became one of the most important myths of modernity.' He then adds: 'now that the secrets of life are ours for the taking we need to ask what role that myth will play in the collective debate about how to make use of them' (Turney, pp. 2–3). It is significant, then, in the context of today's new science of genetics and cloning, along with phenomena such as artificial intelligence, stem cell research, genetically modified food (often called 'Frankenfoods'), and modern plastic surgery, that Turney argues that Shelley's *Frankenstein* remains as vital a text to explore and reinterpret now than it was in the previous two centuries. This recognition of *Frankenstein*'s ongoing influence, and the part it can still play in examining our present relation to science and the futures that science might bring, appears to be based on *Frankenstein*'s radical articulation of the unstable boundaries between the human and the non-human, the natural and the artificial. As Turney states: 'Mary Shelley . . . produced a story which expresses many of the deepest fears and desires about modernity, especially about violation of the body. The human body is both a stable ground for experience in a time of unprecedentedly rapid change and a fragile, limited vessel which we yearn to remake' (Turney, p. 8). Jay Clayton, in an essay which looks at futuristic films such as Ridley Scott's *Blade Runner* (1982) and Steven Spielberg's *A.I.: Artificial Intelligence* (2001), argues that a new reading of *Frankenstein* can be discerned among certain modern artists. This reading, Clayton argues, departs from the traditional one in which the novel mirrors anxieties over a techno-scientific world taking over the human, and reverses it: 'Against all odds, a few influential writers and artists have begun to interpret Shelley's tale of a modern Prometheus as promising things they would like to see happen in real life.' Referencing film-makers like Scott and Spielberg, sci-fi writers like Nancy Kress and Octavia A. Butler and feminist philosophers such as Donna Haraway, Clayton discusses the manner in which these artists and thinkers use 'the legacy of *Frankenstein*, either implicitly or explicitly, to register some positive views of a future containing artificial creatures' (Clayton, p. 85).

Frankenstein is a text which has, ever since it was first published, influenced social and cultural debates over the relationship between human beings, the natural world, and the technological bodies and worlds created by science. In our current age, in which genetics offers the chance of unprecedented alterations in the structure of human life, and in which millions live in environments in which the natural world seems nothing but a memory, it is still a novel which provides a profound myth upon which to build appropriate responses. We must return, once again, to *Frankenstein*'s ability to support both progressive and conservative, optimistic and nostalgic responses to the socio-political world. *Blade Runner*, one of the best sci-fi films to build implicitly from the *Frankenstein* tradition, contains both the optimism and the anxious pessimism described by Clayton. The conflict between Deckard (Harrison Ford) and the replicant Roy Batty (Rutger Hauer) appears in many ways to return us rather precisely to the master–slave dialectic staged in Shelley's novel. There seems here no chance of anything but a battle to the death between human creators and their aspiring but doomed creations. Roy in fact murders his creator in the film; Deckard takes up the baton of pursuit and revenge rather more decisively than does Walton. The film's constant gestures towards environmental breakdown only go to reinforce this pessimistic response to a world in which humanity has become too dependent upon technology and must therefore find a way to control or even kill it. Yet the pathos of Roy's words immediately before his death, and Deckard's union with the beautiful female replicant at the end of the film, seem to point in a different, more positive direction. As Morton puts it:

> Roy, like the creature, is intellectual (beating his maker at chess), literary (quoting lines from Blake's *America* about the fires of Orc), and witty in a creaturely, heavy-handed way. The brilliance of *Blade Runner*, and of *Frankenstein*, is not so much to point out that artificial life and intelligence are possible, but that human life *already is this artificial intelligence*. (Morton, *Frankenstein Sourcebook*, p. 47)

Frankenstein will continue to influence all aspects of culture so long as the boundaries between the human and the artificial, the natural and the technological, are uncertain and in need of intellectual and experimental attention. Its future influence, as a novel and as a myth, has, in other words, as long to run as we do.

CHAPTER 6

FURTHER READING

MODERN SCHOLARLY AND CRITICAL EDITIONS OF
FRANKENSTEIN

There are numerous editions of *Frankenstein* available to readers, but the following are recommended for their scholarly annotations, variants and additional contextual material.

Frankenstein. [1818 text, incorporating 1823 and 1831 variants. Important introductory discussion of the different versions], James Reiger (ed.), 2nd ed. Chicago and London: University of Chicago Press, 1982.

The Mary Shelley Reader. [1818 text, in the context of a selection of Shelley's other works], Betty T. Bennett and Charles E. Robinson (eds). Oxford: Oxford University Press, 1990.

Frankenstein. [1831 text, with appended collation of 1818 and 1831], Maurice Hindle (ed.). London: Penguin Books, 1992.

Frankenstein. [1831 text, with useful appendices on critical reception of the novel], Johanna M. Smith (ed.). Boston: Bedford Books, 1992.

Frankenstein. [1818 text, with collation of 1818 and 1831. Important introductory discussion of the historical contexts behind the scientific aspects of the novel], Marilyn Butler (ed.). Oxford: Oxford University Press, 1994. [Reprinted from William Pickering, 1993]

Frankenstein. [1818 text, with extended endnotes on all known textual variants], Nora Crook (ed.), vol. 1. *The Novels and Selected Works of Mary Shelley*. Nora Crook with Pamela

Clemit (gen. eds), Betty T. Bennett (consulting ed.), 8 vols. London: Pickering and Chatto, 1996.

Frankenstein. [1818 text, with useful appendices], J. Paul Hunter (ed.), Norton Critical Editions. New York: W. W. Norton, 1996.

Frankenstein. [1818 text, with useful contextual material and variants in appendices] D. L. Macdonald and Kathleen Scherf (eds), 2nd ed. Peterborough, Ontario: Broadview Press, 1999.

SOME USEFUL FURTHER READING

There are a huge amount of essays, books and editions on *Frankenstein.* The following works are a good way to begin to study Mary Shelley's novel, her life and her other writings.

Biographies
Seymour, Miranda, *Mary Shelley.* London: John Murray, 2000.
Sunstein, Emily W., *Mary Shelley: Romance and Reality.* Baltimore: The Johns Hopkins University Press, 1989.

Monographs and Essay Collections on Frankenstein
Baldick, Chris, *In Frankenstein's Shadow: Myth, Monstrosity and Nineteenth-Century Writing.* Oxford: The Clarendon Press, 1987.

Botting, Fred, *Making Monstrous: 'Frankenstein', Criticism, Theory.* Manchester and New York: Manchester University Press, 1991.

_____ (ed.), *Frankenstein: Mary Shelley.* London: Macmillan, 1995.

Florescu, Radu, *In Search of Frankenstein: Exploring the Myths Behind Mary Shelley's Monster.* London: Robson Books, 1996.

Forry, Steven Earl, *Hideous Progenies: Dramatizations of 'Frankenstein' from the Nineteenth Century to the Present.* Philadelphia, PA: University of Pennsylvania Press, 1990.

Glut, Donald F., *The Frankenstein Legend: A Tribute to Mary Shelley and Boris Karloff.* Netuchen, NJ: The Scarecrow Press, 1973.

Levine, George and U. C. Knoepflmacher (eds). *The Endurance of 'Frankenstein': Essays on Mary Shelley's Novel*. Berkeley and Los Angeles, CA: University of California Press, 1979.

Morton, Timothy (ed.), *A Routledge Literary Sourcebook on Mary Shelley's 'Frankenstein'*. London and New York: Routledge, 2002.

Schoene-Harwood, Berthold (ed.), *Mary Shelley. 'Frankenstein': A Reader's Guide to Essential Criticism*. Cambridge: Icon Books, 2000.

Monographs and Collections on Mary Shelley's Life and Work

Allen, Graham, *Mary Shelley*. London: Palgrave, 2008.

Bennett, Betty T., *Mary Shelley: An Introduction*. Baltimore and London: The Johns Hopkins University Press, 1998.

Bennett, Betty T. and Stuart Curran (eds), *Mary Shelley in Her Times*. Baltimore and London: The Johns Hopkins University Press, 2000.

Blumberg, Jane, *Mary Shelley's Early Novels: 'This Child of Imagination and Misery'*. London: Macmillan, 1993.

Clemit, Pamela, *The Godwinian Novel: The Rational Fictions of Godwin, Brockden Brown, Mary Shelley*. Oxford: Clarendon Press, 1993.

_____ 'Mary Wollstonecraft Shelley', in *Literature of the Romantic Period: A Bibliographical Guide* Michael O'Neill (ed.), Oxford: Clarendon Press, 1998, pp. 284–97.

Conger, Syndy M., Frederick S. Frank and Gregory O'Dea (eds), *Iconoclastic Departures: Mary Shelley after 'Frankenstein'*. Madison, Teaneck: Fairleigh Dickinson University Press, 1997.

Eberle-Sinatra, Michael, *Mary Shelley's Fictions: From 'Frankenstein' to 'Falkner'*. London: Macmillan, 2000.

Fisch, Audrey A., Anne K. Mellor and Esther H. Schor (eds), *The Other Mary Shelley: Beyond 'Frankenstein'*. New York and Oxford: Oxford University Press, 1993.

Mellor, Anne K., *Mary Shelley: Her Life, Her Fiction, Her Monsters*. New York and London: Routledge, 1989.

Schor, Esther (ed.), *The Cambridge Companion to Mary Shelley*. Cambridge: Cambridge University Press, 2003.

WORKS CITED

Selected Other Works by Mary Shelley

Frankenstein; Or, The Modern Prometheus, 3 vols. London: Lackington, Hughes, Harding, Mavor, and Jones, 1818.

Mary Shelley: Collected Tales and Stories. Charles E. Robinson (ed.). Baltimore and London: The Johns Hopkins University Press, 1976.

The Letters of Mary Wollstonecraft Shelley. Betty T. Bennett (ed.). 3 vols. Baltimore and London: The Johns Hopkins University Press, 1980–8.

The Journals of Mary Shelley. Paula R. Feldman and Diana Scott-Kilvert (eds). Baltimore and London: The Johns Hopkins University Press, 1987; reprinted 1995.

The Novels and Selected Works of Mary Shelley. Nora Crook with Pamela Clemit (gen. eds), Betty T. Bennett (consulting ed.), 8 vols. London: Pickering and Chatto, 1996.

The Frankenstein Notebooks. A Facsimile Edition of Mary Shelley's Manuscript Novel, 1816–17 (With Alterations in the Hand of Percy Bysshe Shelley) as it Survives in Draft and Fair Copy Deposited by Lord Abinger in the Bodleian Library, Oxford (Dep. c. 477/1 and Dep. c. 534/1-2), 2 vols. Charles E. Robinson (ed.), *Manuscripts of the Younger Romantics*, vol. IX. New York and London: Garland Publishing, Inc., 1996.

Mary Shelley's Literary Lives and Other Writings. 4 vols. Nora Crook (ed.). London: Pickering and Chatto, 2002.

Falkner, A Novel. Pamela Clemit (ed.), in Crook and Clemit, *The Novels and Selected Works of Mary Shelley*, vol. 7, op. cit.

The Last Man. Jane Blumberg with Nora Crook (eds), in Crook and Clemit, *The Novels and Selected Works of Mary Shelley*, vol. 4, op. cit.

Lodore. Fiona Stafford (ed.), in Crook and Clemit, *The Novels and Selected Works of Mary Shelley*, vol.6, op. cit.

Mathilda. Pamela Clemit (ed.), in Crook and Clemit, *The Novels and Selected Works of Mary Shelley*, vol.2, op. cit., pp. 1–67.

The Fortunes of Perkin Warbeck, A Romance. Douchet Devin Fischer (ed.), in Crook and Clemit, *The Novels and Selected Works of Mary Shelley*, vol. 5, op. cit.

Rambles in Germany and Italy in 1840, 1842 and 1843. Jeane Moskal (ed.), in Crook and Clemit, *The Novels and Selected Works of Mary Shelley*, vol. 8, op. cit., pp. 61–386.

Valperga: Or, The Life and Adventures of Castruccio, Prince of Lucca. Nora Crook (ed.), in Crook and Clemit, *The Novels and Selected Works of Mary Shelley*, vol. 3, op. cit.

General Studies of Frankenstein *and Mary Shelley*

Adams, Carol, Douglas Buchanan and Kelly Gesch, *The Bedside, Bathtub and Armchair Companion to 'Frankenstein'*. New York and London: Continuum, 2007.

Bann, Stephen (ed.), *Frankenstein, Creation and Monstrosity*. London: Reaktion Books, 1994.

Bloom, Harold (ed.), *Mary Shelley*. New York: Chelsea House, 1985.

_____ (ed.), *Mary Shelley's 'Frankenstein'*. New York: Chelsea House, 1999.

Bunnell, Charlene E., *'All the World's a Stage': Dramatic Sensibility in Mary Shelley's Novels*. New York and London: Routledge, 2002.

Crisafulli, Lilla Maria and Giovanna Silvani (eds), *Mary Versus Mary*. Napoli: Liguori Editore, 2001.

Crook, Nora, 'In Defence of the 1831 *Frankenstein*', in Michael Eberle-Sinatra (ed.) *Mary Shelley's Fictions: From 'Frankenstein' to 'Falkner'*. London: Macmillan, 2000, pp. 3–21.

Dunn, Jane, *Moon in Eclipse: A Life of Mary Shelley*. London: Weidenfield and Nicolson, 1978.

Hill-Miller, Katherine C., *'My Hideous Progeny': Mary Shelley, William Godwin, and the Father–Daughter Relationship*. Newark: University of Delaware Press, 1995.

Ketterer, David, *Frankenstein's Creation: The Book, The Monster, and Human Reality*. Victoria, BC: Victoria University Press, 1979.

Lyles, W. H., *Mary Shelley: An Annotated Bibliography*. New York and London: Garland Publishing, Inc., 1975.

Marshall, Mrs Julian (Florence), *The Life and Letters of Mary Wollstonecraft Shelley*, 2 Vols. London: Richard Bentley and Sons, 1889.

Mulvey-Roberts, Marie and Janet Todd (eds), *Women's Writing*, 6:3 (1999), Special Number, *Mary Shelley*.

Palacio, Jean de, *Mary Shelley dans son oeuvre: Contributions aux études shelleyennes*. Paris: Editions Klincksieck, 1969.

Poovey, Mary, *The Proper Lady and the Woman Writer – Ideology as Style in the Works of Mary Wollstonecraft, Mary Shelley and Jane Austen*. Chicago and London: University of Chicago Press, 1984.

Smith, Johanna M., *Mary Shelley*. New York: Twayne Publishers, 1996.

St Clair, William, *The Godwins and the Shelleys: The Biography of a Family*. London and Boston: Faber and Faber, 1989.

Williams, John, *Mary Shelley: A Literary Life*. London: Macmillan, 2000.

Contexts

Allen, Graham, 'Beyond Biographism: Mary Shelley's *Mathilda*, Intertextuality, and the Wandering Subject', in *Romanticism*, 3.2, 1997. Pamela Clemit (ed.), pp. 170–84.

Barruel, Abbé, *Memoirs Illustrating the History of Jacobinism*, Robert Clifford (trans.). London, 1797–8.

Bennett, Betty, 'The Political Philosophy of Mary Shelley's Historical Novels: *Valperga* and *Perkin Warbeck*', in *The Evidence of the Imagination: Studies of Interactions between Life and Art in English Romantic Literature*. Donald H. Reiman, Michael C. Joyce and Betty T. Bennett with Doucet Devin Fischer and Ricji B. Herzfield (eds.). New York: New York University Press, 1978, pp. 354–71.

Bennett, Betty and Charles E. Robinson (eds), 'Introduction' to *The Mary Shelley Reader*. New York and Oxford: Oxford University Press, 1990, pp. 3–10.

_____ *Mary Diana Dodds: A Gentleman and a Scholar*. Baltimore and London: The Johns Hopkins University Press, 1991.

_____ 'Finding Mary Shelley in Her Letters', in *Romantic Revisions*. Robert Brinkley and Keith Hanley (eds). Cambridge: Cambridge University Press, 1992, pp. 291–306.

_____ 'Feminism and Editing Mary Wollstonecraft Shelley: The Editor And?/Or? The Text', in George Bornstein and

Ralph G. Williams (eds), *Palimpsest: Editorial Theory in the Humanities*. Ann Arbor: University of Michigan Press, 1993, pp. 67–96.

_____ 'Machiavelli's and Mary Shelley's Castruccio: Biography as Metaphor' in *Romanticism*, 3.2, 1997, pp. 139–51.

_____ '"Not this time, Victor": Mary Shelley's Reversioning of Elizabeth, from *Frankenstein* to *Falkner*', in Bennett and Curran, *Mary Shelley in Her Times*, op. cit., pp. 1–17.

Butler, Marilyn, *Romantics, Rebels and Reactionaries: English Literature and its Background, 1760–1830*. Oxford and New York: Oxford University Press, 1981.

_____ (ed.) *Burke, Paine, Godwin and the Revolution Controversy*. Cambridge: Cambridge University Press, 1984.

_____ *Jane Austen and the War of Ideas* 2nd edn. Oxford: Oxford University Press, 1987.

Church, Richard, *Mary Shelley*. London: Gerald Howe, 1928.

Crook, Nora, 'Introduction', in Michael Eberle-Sinatra, *Mary Shelley's Fictions*, op. cit., London: Macmillan, 2000, pp. xix–xxvi.

Dart, Gregory, *Rousseau, Robespierre and English Romanticism*. Cambridge: Cambridge University Press, 1999.

Engelberg, Karsten Klejs, *The Making of the Shelley Myth: An Annotated Bibliography of Criticism of Percy Bysshe Shelley, 1822–1860*. Meckler: Mansell Pubs, 1988.

Gillingham, Lauren, 'Romancing Experience: The Seduction of Mary Shelley's Mathilda', in Studies in *Romanticism*, 42.2, 2003, pp. 251–69.

Hunt, Leigh, *The Autobiography of Leigh Hunt*. J. E. Morpurgo (ed.). London: The Cresset Press, 1949.

Mellor, Anne K. (ed.), *Romanticism and Feminism*. Bloomington and Indianapolis: Indiana University Press, 1988.

_____ *Romanticism and Gender*. New York and London: Routledge, 1993.

Paulson, Ronald, *Representations of Revolution (1789–1820)*. New Haven and London: Yale University Press, 1983.

Philp, Mark, *Godwin's Political Justice*. Ithaca, NY: Cornell University Press, 1986.

Scott, Peter Dale, 'Vital Artifice: Mary, Percy, and the Psychopolitical Integrity of *Frankenstein*', in *The Endurance of 'Frankenstein*', op. cit., p. 172–202.

Shelley, P. B., *The Poems of Shelley*, 2 vols, Geoffrey Matthews and Kelvin Everest (eds). London and New York: Longman, 1989–2000.

St Clair, William, *The Reading Nation in the Romantic Period*. Cambridge: Cambridge University Press, 2004.

Sterrenburg, Lee, 'Mary Shelley's Monster: Politics and Psyche in *Frankenstein*', in *The Endurance of Frankenstein*, op. cit., pp. 143–71.

Trelawny, Edward, *Records of Shelley, Byron, and the Author*, David Wright (eds). Harmondsworth: Penguin, 1973.

_____ *Adventures of a Younger Son* William St Clair (ed.). London: Oxford University Press, 1974.

Language, Form and Style

Austen, Jane, *Northanger Abbey*, Marilyn Butler (ed.). London: Penguin, 1995.

Botting, Fred (ed.), *Gothic*. London and New York: Routledge, 1996.

Bunnell, Charlene E., *'All the World's a Stage': Dramatic Sensibility in Mary Shelley's Novels*. New York and London: Routledge, 2002.

Clery, Emma, *Women's Gothic: From Clara Reeve to Mary Shelley*. Tavistock, Devon: Northcote House, 2000.

Ellis, Kate Ferguson, *The Contested Castle: Gothic Novels and the Subversion of Domestic Ideology*. Urabana: University of Illinois Press, 1989.

Freud, Sigmund, 'The Uncanny', James Strachey (trans.), *The Pelican Freud Library*, vol. 14, *Art and Literature*. Harmondsworth: Penguin, 1985, pp. 335–77.

Godwin, William, *Collected Novels and Memoirs of William Godwin*, 8 vols, Mark Philp (gen. ed.). London: William Pickering, 1992.

Gonda, Caroline, *Reading Daughters' Fictions, 1709–1834: Novels and Society from Manley to Edgeworth*. Cambridge: Cambridge University Press, 1996.

_____ 'Lodore and Fanny Derham's Story', in Women's Writing, 6.3, 1999, pp. 329–44.

Kelly, Gary, The English Jacobin Novel: 1780–1805. Oxford: Clarendon Press, 1976.

_____ English Fiction of the Romantic Period, 1789–1830. London and New York: Longman, 1989.

Kiely, Robert, The Romantic Novel in England. Cambridge, MA: Harvard University Press, 1972.

Lowe-Evans, Mary, Frankenstein: Mary Shelley's Wedding Guest. New York: Twayne Publishers, 1993.

Marshall, David, The Surprising Effects of Sympathy: Marivaux, Diderot, Rousseau, and Mary Shelley. Chicago and London: University of Chicago Press, 1988.

Moskal, Jeanne, ' "To speak in Sanchean phrase": Cervantes and the Politics of Mary Shelley's History of a Six Weeks' Tour', in Bennett and Curran, Mary Shelley in Her Times, op. cit., pp. 18–37.

Mulvey-Roberts, Marie (ed.), The Handbook of Gothic Literature. London: Macmillan, 1998.

Punter, David, The Literature of Terror: A History of Gothic Fictions from 1765 to the Present Day, 2 vols. London and New York: Longman, 1996.

Rajan, Tilottama, The Supplement of Reading: Figures of Understanding in Romantic Theory and Practice. Ithaca and London: Cornell University Press, 1990.

Richardson, Alan, Literature, Education and Romanticism: Reading as a Social Practice, 1780–1832. Cambridge: Cambridge University Press, 1994.

Royle, Nicholas, The Uncanny. London and New York: Routledge, 2003.

Scrivener, Michael, 'Frankenstein's Ghost Story: The Last Jacobin Novel', in Genre, 19.3, 1986, pp. 299–318.

Shelley, P. B., The Letters of Percy Bysshe Shelley, 2 vols, Frederick L. Jones (ed.). Oxford: Clarendon Press, 1964.

Webster-Garrett, Erin L., The Literary Career of Novelist Mary Shelley After 1822: Romance, Realism, and the Politics of Gender. Lewiston, Queenston, Lampeter: The Edwin Mellon Press, 2006.

Wollstonecraft, Mary, *'Mary' and 'The Wrongs of Woman'*, Gary Kelly (ed.). Oxford: Oxford University Press, 1976.

Reading Frankenstein

Allen, Graham, 'Godwin, Fénelon, and the Disappearing Teacher', in *History of Europan Ideas*, 33, 2007, pp. 9–24.

_____ ' "Unfashioned creatures, but half made up": Beginning with Mary Shelley's Spectre', in *Angelaki*, 12:3, 2008, forthcoming.

Blake, William, *William Blake: The Complete Illuminated Books*. David Bindman (ed.). London: Thames and Hudson, 2000.

Byron, George Gordon (Lord), *The Major Works*, Jerome J. McGann (ed.). Oxford and New York: Oxford University Press, 1986.

Coleridge, S. T., *Poems*, John Beer (ed.). London: Dent, 1993.

Derrida, Jacques, *The Politics of Friendship*, George Collins (trans.). London and New York: Verso, 1997.

Godwin, William, *Memoirs of the Author of A Vindication of the Rights of Woman* and Mary Wollstonecraft, *Letters Written During a Short Residence in Sweden, Norway, and Denmark*, Richard Holmes (ed.). London: Penguin, 1987.

Gordon, Lyndall, *Mary Wollstonecraft: A New Genus*. London: Little, Brown, 2005.

McWhir, Anne, 'Teaching the Monster to Read: Mary Shelley's Education and *Frankenstein*', in *The Educational Legacy of Romanticism*, John Willinsky (ed.). Waterloo, Ontario: Wilfrid Laurier University Press, 1990, pp. 73–92.

Milton, John, *Paradise Lost*, Gordon Teskey (ed.). New York and London: W. W. Norton and Co., 2005.

Rousseau, Jean-Jacques, *Émile*, Barbara Foxley (trans.). London: Dent, 1993.

Todd, Janet, *Mary Wollstonecraft: A Revolutionary Life*. London: Weidenfeld and Nicolson, 2000.

Veeder, William, *Mary Shelley and 'Frankenstein'*. Chicago: University of Chicago Press, 1986.

Volney, C. F. C. (Comte de), *The Ruins: or A Survey of the Revolutions of Empires*. London: J. Johnson, 1796.

Wollstonecraft, Mary, *A Vindication of the Rights of Man and A Vindication of the Rights of Woman*, D. L. Macdonald and Kathleen Scherf (eds). Peterborough, Ontario: Broadview Press, 1997.

Zonana, Joyce, ' "They Will Prove the Truth of My Tale": Safie's Letters as a Feminist Core of Mary Shelley's *Frankenstein*', in *The Journal of Narrative Technique*, 21, 1991, pp. 170–84.

Critical Reception, Composition and Publishing History

[anon. review of *Frankenstein*], *La Belle Assemblée, or Court and Fashionable Magazine*, 2nd series, 17, March 1818, in Reiman, *Romantics Reviewed*, vol. 1, op. cit., pp. 42–5.

[anon. review of *Frankenstein*], *The British Critic*. n.s. 9, April 1818, pp. 432–8.

[anon. review of *Frankenstein*], in *The Edinburgh Magazine and Literary Miscellany, A New Series of the Scots Magazine*. 2, March 1818, in *Frankenstein*, D. L. Macdonald and Kathleen Scherf (eds), op. cit., pp. 306–8.

[anon. review of *Frankenstein*], in *The Literary Panorama, and National Register*. n.s., 8, June 1818, pp. 411–14.

[anon. review of *Frankenstein*], in *The Monthly Review, or Literary Journal*. n.s., 85, April 1818, p. 439.

Bohls, Elizabeth A., *Women Travel Writers and the Language of Aesthetics, 1716–1818*. Cambridge: Cambridge University Press, 1995.

Crocker, John Wilson, review of *Frankenstein* in *The Quarterly Review*, 18, January 1818, in *Frankenstein*, D. L. Macdonald and Kathleen Scherf (eds), op. cit., pp. 306–8.

Godwin, William, *Political and Philosophical Writings of William Godwin*, 7 vols, Mark Philp (gen. ed.). London: William Pickering, 1993.

Leader, Zacharay, 'Parenting *Frankenstein*', in *Revision and Romantic Authorship*. Oxford: Clarendon Press, 1996, pp. 167–205

Mellor, Anne K., 'Choosing a Text of *Frankenstein* to Teach', in *Approaches to Teaching Shelley's 'Frankenstein'*, Stephen C. Behrendt (ed.). New York: The Modern Language Association of America, 1990, pp. 31–7.

Murray, E. B., 'Shelley's Contribution to Mary's *Frankenstein*' in *The Keats-Shelley Memorial Bulletin*. 29, 1978, pp. 50–68.

'Changes in the 1823 Edition of *Frankenstein*', in *The Library*, 6th Series, 3, 1981, pp. 320–7.

O'Rourke, James, 'The 1831 Introduction and Revisions to *Frankenstein*: Mary Shelley Dictates Her Legacy', in *Studies in Romanticism*. 38, Fall 1999, pp. 365–85.

Reiman, Donald (ed.), *The Romantics Reviewed: Contemporary Reviews of British Romantic Writers*, Part C. *Shelley, Keats, and London Radical Writers*, 2 vols. New York and London: Garland Publishing, 1972.

Adaptation, Interpretation and Influence

i. Frankenstein *Stage Adaptations*

Anon, *Frank-in-Steam; or, The Modern Promise to Pay* (1824), in Forry, *Hideous Progenies*, op. cit., pp. 177–86.

Brough, Richard and Barnabus, *Frankenstein; or, The Model Man* (1846), in Forry, op. cit., pp. 227–50.

Kerr, John Atkinson, *The Monster and the Magician; or, The Fate of Frankenstein* (1826), in Forry, op. cit., pp. 205–26.

Milner, Henry M., *Frankenstein; or, The Man and the Monster* (1826), in Forry, op. cit., pp. 187–204.

Peake, Richard Brinsley, *Presumption; or, The Fate of Frankenstein* (1823), in Forry, op. cit., pp. 135–60.

Peake, Richard Brinsley, *Another Piece of Presumption* (1823), in Forry, op. cit., pp. 161–76.

ii. Frankenstein *Films*

Abbott and Costello Meet Frankenstein, Erle C. Kenton (dir.). Universal Pictures, USA, 1945.

Andy Warhol's Frankenstein [Flesh for Frankenstein], Paul Morrissey (and Antonio Margheriti) (dir.). EMI, USA, 1973.

The Bride of Frankenstein, James Whale (dir.). Universal Pictures, USA, 1935.

The Curse of Frankenstein, Terence Fisher (dir.). Hammer Films, UK, 1957.

The Evil of Frankenstein, Terence Fisher (dir.). Hammer Films, UK, 1964.

Frankenstein, James Whale (dir.). Universal Pictures, USA, 1931.

Frankenstein and the Monster from Hell, Terence Fisher (dir.). Hammer Films, 1974.

Frankenstein Created Woman, Terence Fisher (dir.). Hammer Films, UK, 1967.

Frankenstein Meets the Wolfman, Roy William Neil (dir.). Universal Pictures, USA, 1943.

Frankenstein Must Be Destroyed, Terence Fisher (dir.). Hammer Films, UK, 1969.

Frankenstein Unbound, Roger Corman (dir.). Warner Bros/ Mount Company, USA, 1990.

The Ghost of Frankenstein, Erle C. Kenton (dir.). Universal Pictures, USA, 1942.

Gothic, Ken Russell (dir.). Virgin Vision, UK, 1986.

Horror of Frankenstein, Jimmy Sangster (dir.). Hammer Films, UK, 1970.

House of Frankenstein, Erle C. Kenton (dir.). Universal Pictures, USA, 1944.

Life Without Soul, Joseph W. Smiley (dir.). Ocean Film Corporation, USA, 1915.

Mary Shelley's 'Frankenstein', Kenneth Branagh (dir.). American Zoetrop, TriStar Pictures, USA, 1994.

The Revenge of Frankenstein, Terence Fisher (dir.). Hammer Films, UK, 1958.

The Rocky Horror Picture Show, Jim Sharman (dir.). Twentieth-Century Fox, USA, 1975.

Son of Frankenstein, Rowland V. Lee (dir.). Universal Pictures, USA, 1939.

Young Frankenstein, Mel Brooks (dir.). Twentieth-Century Fox/Gruskoff-Venture Films, USA, 1974.

iii. Other Films

A. I. Artificial Intelligence, Steven Spielberg (dir.). DreamWorks Pictures, 2001.

Blade Runner, Ridley Scott (dir.). Ladd Company, USA, 1982.

Carry on Screaming, Gerald Thomas (dir.). CANAL+ Image UK, 1966.

Four Sided Triangle, Terence Fisher (dir.). Hammer Films, UK, 1953.
The Golem [Orig. *Der Golem Wie Er In Die Welt Kam*], Paul Wegener and Carol Boese (dirs). Pagu/UFA, Germany, 1920.
Metropolis, Fritz Lang (dir.). UFA, Germany, 1926.

iv. Interpretations and Further Reading
Aldiss, Brian, *Frankenstein Unbound: A Novel*. New York: Random House, 1973.
Barthes, Roland, *Camera Lucida: Reflections on Photography*, Richard Howard (trans.). New York: Hill and Wang, 1981.
Bewell, Alan, 'An Issue of Monstrous Desire: *Frankenstein* and Obstetrics', *Yale Journal of Criticism*, 2, 1988, pp. 105–28.
Bohls, Elizabeth A., 'Standards of Taste, Discourses of "Race", and the Aesthetic Education of a Monster: Critique of Empire in *Frankenstein*', *Eighteenth-Century Life*, 18.3, 1994, pp. 23–36.
Bronfen, Elizabeth, 'Rewriting the Family: Mary Shelley's "Frankenstein" in its Biographical/Textual Context', in Bann, *Frankenstein, Creation and Monstrosity*, op. cit., pp. 16–38.
Brooks, Peter, '"Godlike Science/Unhallowed Arts": Language, Nature, and Monstrosity', in *The Endurance of 'Frankenstein'*, op. cit., pp. 205–20 [also in Harold Bloom, *Mary Shelley*, op. cit., pp. 101–14].
_____ 'What is a Monster? (According to *Frankenstein*)', in Botting, *Frankenstein: Mary Shelley*, op. cit., pp. 81–106.
Carson, James P., 'Bringing the Author Forward: *Frankenstein* through Mary Shelley's Letters', *Criticism*, 30.4 (1988), pp. 431–53.
Clayton, Jay, '*Frankenstein*'s futurity: replicants and robots', in Schor, *Cambridge Companion to Mary Shelley*, op. cit., pp. 84–99.
Collings, David, 'The Monster and the Imaginary Mother: A Lacanian Reading of *Frankenstein*', in Smith, *Frankenstein*, op. cit., pp. 245–58.
Ellis, Kate, 'Monsters in the Garden: Mary Shelley and the Bourgeois Family', in *The Endurance of 'Frankenstein'*, op. cit., pp. 123–42.
Freeman, Barbara Claire, '*Frankenstein* with Kant: A Theory of

Monstrosity or the Monstrosity of Theory', in Botting, *Frankenstein: Mary Shelley*, op. cit., pp. 191–205.

Frentz, Thomas S. and Janice H. Rushing, 'The *Frankenstein* Myth in Contemporary Cinema', in William Nothshine, Carole Blair and Gary A. Copeland (eds), *Critical Questions: Invention, Creativity, and the Criticism of Discourse and Media*. New York: St. Martin's Press, 1994, pp. 155–82.

Gilbert, Sandra M. and Susan Gubar, 'Horror's Twin: Mary Shelley's Monstrous Eve', in *The Madwoman in the Attic: The Woman Writer and the Nineteenth-Century Literary Imagination*. New Haven and London: Yale University Press, 1979, pp. 213–47.

Grant, Michael, 'James Whale's *Frankenstein*: The Horror Film and the Symbolic Biology of the Cinematic Monster', in Bann, *Frankenstein, Creation and Monstrosity*, op. cit., pp. 113–35.

Griffin, Andrew, 'Fire and Ice in *Frankenstein*', in *The Endurance of 'Frankenstein'*, op. cit., pp. 49–73.

Habermas, Jurgen, 'Modernity: An Incomplete Project' in Peter Brooker (ed.), *Modernism/Postmodernism*. London and New York: Longman, 1992, pp. 125–38.

Hammond, Raymond, *The Modern Frankenstein: Fiction Becomes Fact*. Poole: Blandford, 1986.

Hatlin, Burton, 'Milton, Mary Shelley, and Patriarchy', *Bucknell Review*. 28, 1983, pp. 19–47.

Heller, Lee E., '*Frankenstein* and the Cultural Uses of Gothic', in Smith, *Frankenstein*, op. cit., pp. 325–41.

Hobbs, Colleen, 'Reading the Symptoms: An Exploration of Repression and Hysteria in Mary Shelley's *Frankenstein*', *Studies in the Novel*, 25.2, 1993, pp. 152–69.

Hodges, Devon, '*Frankenstein* and the Feminine Subversion of the Novel', *Tulsa Studies in Women's Literature*, 2.2, 1983, pp. 155–64.

Hoeveler, Diane Long, '*Frankenstein*, feminism, and literary theory', in Schor, *Cambridge Companion to Mary Shelley*, op. cit., pp. 45–62.

Hogle, Jerrold E., 'Otherness in *Frankenstein*: The

Confinement/Autonomy of Fabrication', in Botting, *Frankenstein: Mary Shelley*, op. cit., pp. 206–34.

Homans, Margaret, 'Bearing Demons: Frankenstein's Circumvention of the Maternal', in Botting, *Frankenstein: Mary Shelley*, op. cit., pp. 140–65.

Hutchings, Peter, *Terence Fisher*. Manchester: Manchester University Press, 2001.

Jacobus, Mary, 'Is There a Woman in This Text?', *New Literary History*, 14.1, 1982, pp. 117–41.

James, Louis, 'Frankenstein's Monster in Two Traditions' in Bann, *Frankenstein, Creation and Monstrosity*, op. cit., pp. 77–94.

Johnson, Barbara, 'My Monster/My Self', in *A World of Difference*. Baltimore and London: The Johns Hopkins University Press, 1987, pp. 144–54.

Jones, Darryl, *Horror: A Thematic History in Fiction and Film*. London: Arnold, 2002.

Jones, Stephen, *The 'Frankenstein' Scrapbook: The Complete Movie Guide to the World's Most Famous Monster*. New York: Citadel Press, 1995.

Kestner, Joseph, 'Narcissism as Symptom and Structure: The Case of Mary Shelley's *Frankenstein*', in Botting, *Frankenstein: Mary Shelley*, op. cit., pp. 68–80.

Knoepflmacher, U. C., 'Thoughts on the Aggression of Daughters', in *The Endurance of 'Frankenstein'*, op. cit., pp. 88–119.

Lavalley, Albert J., 'The Stage and Film Children of *Frankenstein*: A Survey', in *The Endurance of 'Frankenstein'*, op. cit., pp. 243–89.

Leggett, Paul, *Terence Fisher: Horror, Myth and Religion*. Jefferson, North Carolina and London: MacFarland & Company, Inc., 2002.

Levine, George, 'The Ambiguous Heritage of *Frankenstein*', in *The Endurance of 'Frankenstein'*, op. cit., pp. 3–30.

_____ '*Frankenstein* and the Tradition of Realism', in Bloom, *Mary Shelley*, op. cit., pp. 81–99.

Lowe-Evans, Mary, 'Reading with a "Nicer Eye": Responding to *Frankenstein*', in Smith, *Frankenstein*, op. cit., pp. 215–29.

McCarty, John, *Hammer Films*. Harpenden, Herts: Pocket Essentials, 2002.

Malchow, H. L., 'Frankenstein's Monster and Images of Race in Nineteenth-Century Britain', *Past and Present*, 139, 1993, pp. 90–130.

Marshall, Tim, *Murdering to Dissect: Graverobbing, 'Frankenstein', and the Anatomy of Literature*. Manchester: Manchester University Press, 1995.

Moers, Ellen, 'Female Gothic', in *The Endurance of 'Frankenstein'*, op. cit., pp. 77–87.

Montag, Warren, "The Workshop of Filthy Creation': A Marxist Reading of *Frankenstein*', in Smith, *Frankenstein*, op. cit., pp. 300–11.

Morton, Timothy, *Shelley and the Revolution in Taste: The Body and the Natural World*. Cambridge: Cambridge University Press, 1994.

Myers, Mitzi, 'Mary Wollstonecraft Godwin Shelley: The Female Author between Public and Private Spheres', in Bennett and Curran, *Mary Shelley in Her Times*, op. cit., pp. 160–72.

Nelson, Jr, Lowry, 'Night Thoughts on the Gothic Novel', in Bloom, *Mary Shelley*, op. cit., pp. 31–48.

Nestrick, William, 'Coming to Life: *Frankenstein* and the Nature of Film Narrative', in *The Endurance of 'Frankenstein'*, op. cit., pp. 290–315.

Newman, Beth, 'Narratives of Seduction and the Seductions of Narrative: The Frame Structure of *Frankenstein*', in Botting, *Frankenstein: Mary Shelley*, op. cit., pp. 166–90.

O'Flinn, Paul, 'Production and Reproduction: The Case of *Frankenstein*', in Botting, *Frankenstein: Mary Shelley*, op. cit., pp. 21–47.

O'Rourke, James, ' "Nothing More Unnatural" : Mary Shelley's Revision of Rousseau', *English Literary History*, 35.1, 1989, pp. 543–69.

Paulson, Ronald, 'Gothic Fiction and the French Revolution', *English Literary History*, 48.3, 1981, pp. 532–54.

Pirie, David, *A Heritage of Horror: The English Gothic Cinema 1946–1972*. London: Gordon Fraser, 1973.

Rauch, Alan, 'The Monstrous Body of Knowledge in Mary

Shelley's *Frankenstein*', *Studies in Romanticism*, 34.2, 1995, pp. 227–53.

Schor, Esther, '*Frankenstein* and Film', in Schor, *Cambridge Companion to Mary Shelley*, op. cit., pp. 63–83.

Sedgwick, Eve Kosofsky, *Between Men: English Literature and Homosocial Desire*. New York: Columbia University Press, 1985.

Sherwin, Paul, '*Frankenstein*: Creation and Catastrophe', in Bloom, *Mary Shelley*, op. cit., pp. 137–67.

Smith, Johanna M., ' "Cooped Up": Feminine Domesticity in *Frankenstein*', in Smith, *Frankenstein*, op. cit., pp. 270–85.

Spark, Muriel, '*Frankenstein*', in Bloom, *Mary Shelley*, op. cit., pp. 11–30.

Spivak, Gayatri Chakravorty, 'Three Women's Texts and a Critique of Imperialism', in Botting, *Frankenstein: Mary Shelley*, op. cit., pp. 235–60.

Stevick, Philip, '*Frankenstein* and Comedy', in *The Endurance of 'Frankenstein'*, op. cit., pp. 221–39.

Turney, Jon, *Frankenstein's Footsteps: Science, Genetics and Popular Culture*. New Haven and London: Yale University Press, 1998.

Walling, William, 'Victor Frankenstein's Dual Role', in Bloom, *Mary Shelley*, op. cit., pp. 57–64.

Wilt, Judith, '*Frankenstein* as Mystery Play', in *The Endurance of 'Frankenstein'*, op. cit., pp. 31–48.

INDEX